Fine WoodWorking

DESIGN
BOOK
SIX

Fine WoodWorking®

DESIGN BOOK SIX

266 photographs
of the best work
in wood

Introduction by
Sandor Nagyszalanczy

With an essay
by Scott Landis
on apprenticeship

The Taunton Press

Front-cover photograph:
RICHARD L. FORD, JR.
San Diego, Calif.

"Hal & Stewart"
(see p. 62)
Photo by Dean Powell

Back-cover photographs:
BONNIE KLEIN
Renton, Wash.

Chatterwork spin tops
(see p. 143)
Photo by Mustafa Bilal

DAN MOSHEIM
Arlington, Vt.

Gent's chest
(see p. 6)
Photo by Cook Neilson

DENIS J. SEMPREBON, STEVE
NYSTROM and WILL NEPTUNE
Stow, Mass.

Traditional mantelpiece
(see p. 104)
Photo by Lance Patterson

TAUNTON
BOOKS&VIDEOS

...by fellow enthusiasts

© 1992 by The Taunton Press, Inc.
All rights reserved

First printing: April 1992
Printed in the United States of America

A FINE WOODWORKING Book

FINE WOODWORKING® is a trademark of The Taunton Press, Inc.,
registered in the U.S. Patent and Trademark Office.

The Taunton Press, 63 South Main Street, Box 5506,
Newtown, CT 06470-5506

Library of Congress Cataloging-in-Publication Data

Fine woodworking design book six : 266 photographs of the best
     work in wood / introduction by Sandor Nagyszalanczy : essay by
     Scott Landis on apprenticeship.
          p.   cm.
     ISBN 1-56158-017-1
          1. Furniture — United States — History — 20th century — Catalogs.
     2. Decorative arts — United States — History — 20th century — Catalogs.
     3. Wood-carving — United States — History — 20th century — Catalogs.
     I. Landis, Scott.   II. Fine woodworking.   III Title: Fine
     woodworking design book 6.
     NK2408.F58 1992   92-4126
     674'.8 — dc20   CIP

Contents

Introduction

When I was asked to guide the selection process for *Design Book Six,* I knew the nature of the challenge; I've taken part in the judging of the last two design books. I knew how gargantuan the volume of entries would be (we'd sifted through more than 10,000 color transparencies for *Design Book Five).* I knew that it would take dozens of hours to scrutinize that mountain of images and reduce it to a molehill of finalists. However, I also knew I was in for one of the greatest treats a woodworking enthusiast could have: to preview one of the finest collections of contemporary furniture anywhere.

Woodworkers who took the challenge and sent in photos of their work then ran the gauntlet of our judging process, which selected about one finalist for every 32 images received. To keep the process from being limited by our subjective whims, all members of the *Fine Woodworking* staff who participated in the judging tried hard to be objective and consider each entry's technical and design merits above their personal tastes. No one rejected a piece simply because it wouldn't look good in their living room. We tried to select the best work that fit our goal of creating a contemporary portrait of woodworking. That means that much of the work displays originality in overall form, construction or use of materials. But as well as illustrating the "cutting edge" of woodworking, the collection serves to represent a wide range of styles, including work that exemplifies identifiable periods and styles. In a few instances we've included a reproduction period piece because it is, in our opinion, an example of some of the finest work that we've seen in that genre.

After reviewing over 8,000 slides, here's a brief summary of what I would say are trends in contemporary woodworking. First of all, our collective romance with polychrome (painted or plastic-laminate covered) woodworking has died down. But it's not out entirely. Makers are using colors more judiciously to enhance their pieces, sometimes by adding small splashes of color juxtaposed with clear finished wood as an accent; sometimes by tinting to alter the tone, and hence the feeling, of natural wood. At the other end, highly figured woods are also being used less flagrantly and more judiciously. When they are used, makers often incorporate them as focal points or highlights in a piece, such as fiddleback-grained panels surrounded by plain-wood frames, rather than employing them to overwhelm the viewer with their visual busyness. Joinery as well has come a long way since the days when prominently exposed dovetails and through-mortised-and-pinned tenons were de rigueur on casework and furniture. Joinery is more commonly hidden now, taking a back seat to the piece's overall form. This trend is partially owing to new technologies, such as plate joinery, that make strong, quick hidden joints possible, and to makers who often incorporate curved elements in their work that don't lend themselves as well to exposed joints.

What makes *Design Book Six* different from previous design books? Woodworkers, both professional and amateur, seem to be paying more attention to developing well-proportioned forms, as well as integrating the details of a piece rather than just tacking them on. The results display more innovative edge treatments, motifs, surface decorations, finishes and hardware. These pieces show a greater confidence and command of both visual and technical ability than I've seen before. The extremely competitive nature of the selection process makes this publication the best Taunton Press design book ever. Whether you peruse these pages to observe the work of your peers and to glean ideas from some of the most innovative makers of the day or just to delight at the beauty of so many dreams "tree ripened" to reality, may your life and work be enriched by the spirit of these creations.

Sandor Nagyszalanczy
Managing Editor,
Fine Woodworking magazine

Cabinets

LARRY TEMPLETON
Dallas, Tex.

Leaded-glass cabinet
Walnut, walnut crotch veneer
34 in. x 13 in. x 56 in.
Photo by Cutter-Smith
Photographics

STEPHEN TURINO
Wakefield, R.I.

TV/stereo cabinet
Sapele, Aura Vera,
Gaboon ebony
128 in. x 24 in. x 48 in.
Photo by Ric Murray

BRIAN BEARD
Modesto, Calif.

Wall cabinet
Maple, ipe, German blown glass
18 in. x 6 in. x 28 in.
Photo by Cory Warner

JON ALLEY
Churchville, Pa.

"A Small Place in the Country"
Honduras mahogany,
maple plywood, birch
plywood, apple, marble
31 in. x 15 in. x 42 in.
Photo by Jon Alley

JOEL EVETT and
ROBERTA BOYLEN
Belmont, Mass.

"Aesop Box: The Wolf and the
Lamb" and "Aesop Box: The
Fox and the Grapes"
Walnut, macassar ebony,
cherry, rosewood, poplar,
egg tempra, abalone shell,
fresh-water pearl
21 in. x 11 in. x 32 in.
Photo by A. Dean Powell

DAN MOSHEIM
Arlington, Vt.

Gent's chest
Cherry, pine
42 in. x 24 in. x 66 in.
Photo by Cook Neilson

DANIEL BOTHE
Jamesville, N.Y.

China cabinet
Curly maple, purpleheart, brass
40 in. x 14 in. x 86 in.
Photo by Douglas Manchee

JEFFREY WASSERMAN
Swampscott, Mass.

Console cabinet
Bird's-eye maple, plywood,
paint, graphite
60 in. x 22 in. x 39 in.
Photo by James Beards

DAN BOLLINGER
West Lafayette, Ind.

"Tommy"
Birch, Baltic birch, pine
20 in. x 16 in. x 50 in.
Photo by Dan Bollinger

JOSHUA GOLDBERG
Dartmouth, Mass.

Coat closet
Poplar, plywood, copper,
rice paper
16 in. x 19 in. x 84 in.
Photo by Dean Powell

GREG ZALL
Ft. Bragg, Calif.

Linen cabinet
Fir, doussié, basswood
25 in. x 12 in. x 53 in.
Photo by Sean Sprague

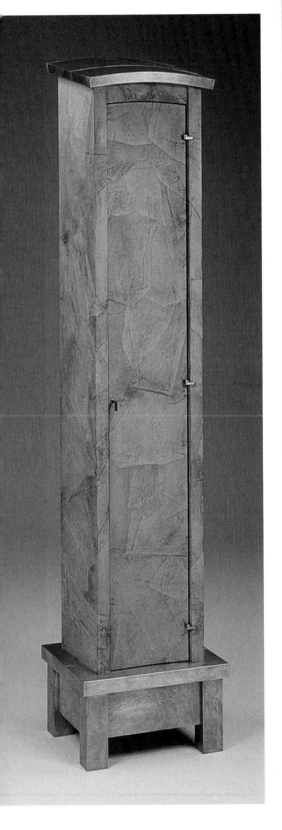

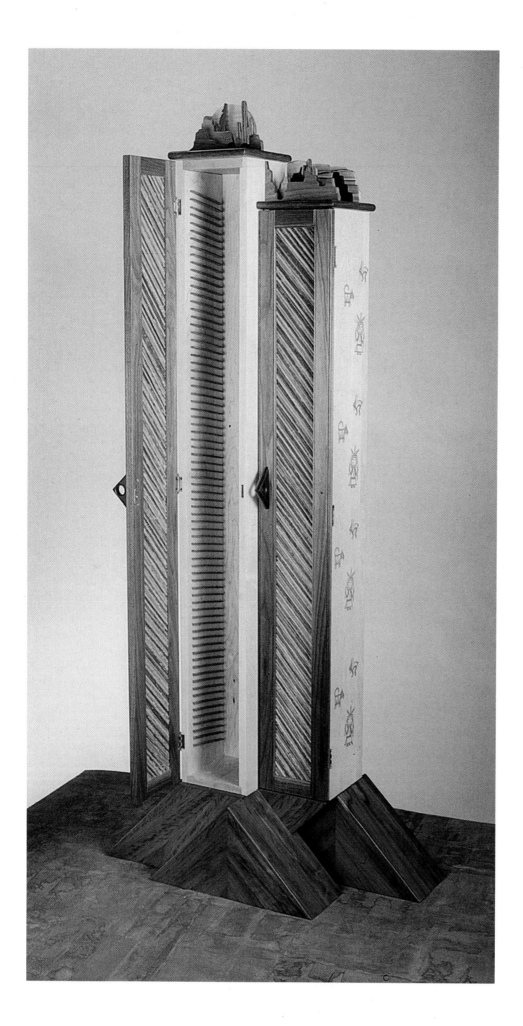

VICTOR CLAPP
Edmonton, Alberta, Canada

Compact-disc tower
Maple, walnut, padauk,
silk screen
30 in. x 14 in. x 66 in.
Photo by Michael Shimbashi

BARBARA GOODWIN
Haverstraw, N.Y.

Piano cabinet
(Detail above right)
Cherry, lacquer
42 in. x 13 in. x 9 in.
Photo by Barbara Goodwin

10

SUSAN PFEIFFER
Elizabethtown, Ky.

"There Were Whales"
Wall cabinet
Ebonized cherry, basswood
15 in. x 18 in. x 36 in.
Photo by Scott Mitchell

JON SHAW
Badminton, Avon, England

Textile-collection cabinet
Burr walnut, wenge
18¼ in. x 48¼ in. x 83½ in.
Photo by Blantern & Davis

JOHN SCHWARTZKOPF
Cedar Rapids, Iowa

Bevel-front entertainment center
Padauk, curly bubinga,
rosewood, curly maple
45 in. x 18 in. x 38 in.
Photo by Rod Bradley

STEVEN HOLMAN
Dorset, Vt.

Sideboard
French walnut veneer,
walnut, padauk, ash
36 in. x 16 in. x 38 in.
Photo by Cook Neilson

MICHAEL McALEENAN
Gloucester, Mass.

"Sheratonesque Sideboard"
Mahogany, pine, poplar
57 in. x 24 in. x 41 in.
Photo by Lance Patterson

ROBERT DIEMERT
Greensville, Ontario, Canada

"Arthur's Armoire"
Macassar ebony, bubinga,
mother-of-pearl
60 in. x 24 in. x 75 in.
Photo by Jeremy Jones

THOMAS HUGH STANGELAND
Seattle, Wash.

Collectors cabinet
Brazilian rosewood, louro
preto, ebony, sycamore, brass
34 in. x 15 in. x 68 in.
Photo by Anil Kapahi

MICHAEL BARTELL
Pine, Ariz.

Hutch
Peruvian walnut, cherry
58 in. x 18 in. x 78 in.
Photo by Gene Sasse

JAN VOKSNERA
Chino Valley, Ariz.

Entertainment unit
Maple, satiné, ebony
108 in. x 16 in. x 96 in.
Photo by Jan Voksnera

JOHN and LAURA LUSH
Yuba City, Calif.

Bow-front display case
Goncalo alves, wenge
37 in. x 14 in. x 48 in.
Photo by Tom Upton

STEVEN L. MIDKIFF
Cincinnati, Ohio

Entertainment center/dry bar
Black walnut, claro walnut,
maple burl
123 in. x 24 in. x 81 in.
Photo by Richard H. Binstadt

LOY DAVIS MARTIN
Palo Alto, Calif.

Sideboard
(Detail at right)
Swiss pear, figured bubinga,
Brazilian rosewood
96 in. x 19 in. x 35 in.
Photo by Paul Fairchild

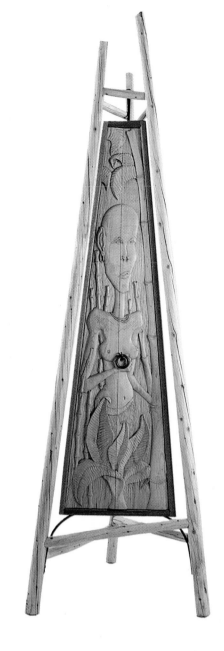

MICHAEL FRATRICK
Albuquerque, N. Mex.

China cabinet
Wenge, mahogany
54 in. x 16 in. x 84 in.
Photo by Alan Labb

SCOTT RIKKERS
Ophir, Colo.

Standing cabinet
Mahogany, maple, pine
26 in. x 26 in. x 84 in.
Photo by Deborah Ford

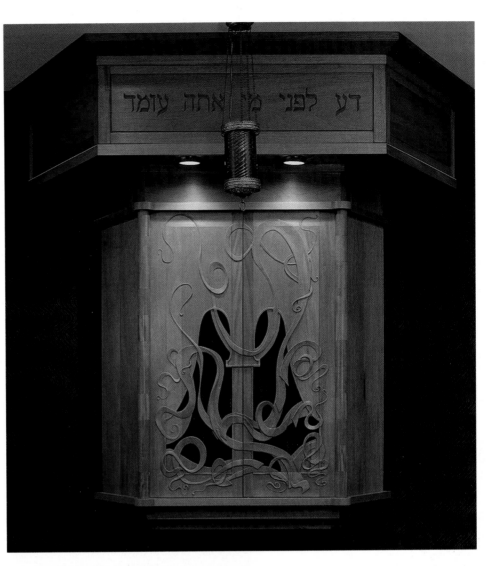

ROBERT A. SPANGLER and
ALAN WEINSTEIN
Seattle, Wash.

Torah ark
Mahogany
96 in. x 24 in. x 96 in.
Photo by Mark Tade

STEPHEN KLEBS
Grandview, N.Y.

"California Credenza"
Cherry
78 in. x 14 in. x 28¼ in.
Photo by Cheryl Klauss

IRA A. KEER and
BRUCE KIEFFER
Minneapolis, Minn.

"T. Squares: An Armoire"
Curly maple, ebonized walnut,
brazilwood, tinted glass
34 in. x 22½ in. x 73½ in.
Photo by Bill Zuehlke

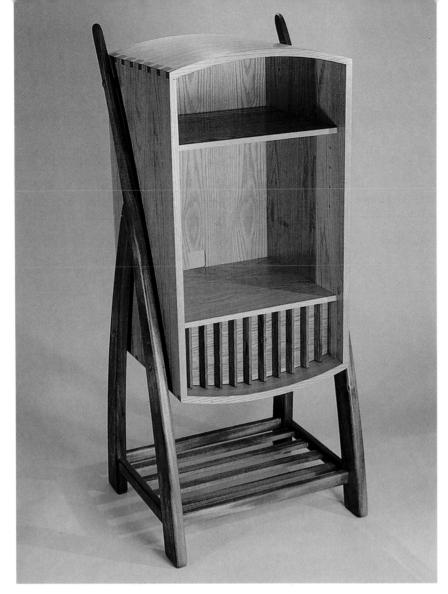

RANDY DeBEY
Fort Collins, Colo.

Stereo cabinet
Red oak, Honduras mahogany
20⅝ in. x 23⅛ in. x 51⅝ in.
Photo by Bill Scherer

JANET SHAFER
Staunton, Va.

"Rain Cabinet"
Cherry, maple, black dye
29 in. x 16 in. x 71¼ in.
Photo by Janet Shafer

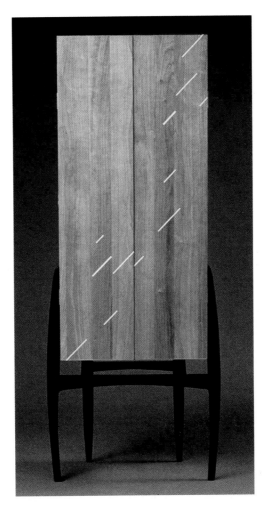

MICHAEL CLAPPER
Lansing, N.Y.

"Anasazi Cabinet"
European beech veneer,
painted plywood, glass
13 in. x 23 in. x 84 in.
Photo by David Mohney

GEORGE GORDON
Rehoboth, Mass.

Sideboard
Figured walnut, black walnut,
white ash
78 in. x 28 in. x 34 in.
Photo by Douglas Dalton
Photography

KIMBERLY A. KELZER
Oakland, Calif.

"Home on the Range"
Plywood, poplar, aluminum,
Plexiglas, Corian, silicone
21 in. x 26 in. x 45 in.
Photo by Kimberly A. Kelzer

RALF KEELER
Seattle, Wash.

"Ancient River, Modern Man"
Stereo cabinet
Bubinga, maple, wenge,
bird's-eye maple
24 in. x 18 in. x 77 in.
Photo by Stan Shockey

BRUCE PETERSON
Embudo, N. Mex.

Mountain columbine cabinet
Black walnut, juniper, cholla
cactus, tamarisk reeds
42 in. x 18 in. x 56 in.
Photo by Ernest Leroy Salazar

CARL DIMON and
GLENN E. HUGHES
Bedminster, Pa./Revere, Pa.

China cabinet
Cherry, ebony, bird's-eye maple
98 in. x 32 in. x 94 in.
Photo by Mitch Mandel

RICK BRUNNER
Baton Rouge, La.

Buffet cabinet
Padauk, Baltic birch, ebony,
silver, brass, pigments
90 in. x 20 in. x 36 in.
Photo by Robert Davis

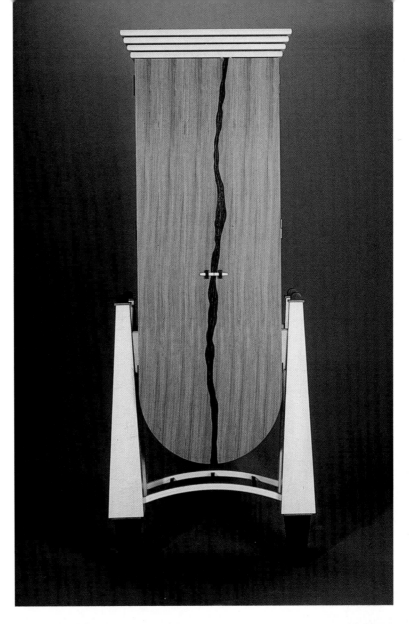

Chairs &
Benches

STEPHEN DANIELL
Easthampton, Mass.

"Icarus Chair"
Cherry, maple,
dyed black veneer
27 in. x 32 in. x 36 in.
Photo by Bob Barrett

D. LEO FLYNN
Lake Charles, La.

"Womb Rocker II"
Baltic-birch plywood
48 in. x 33 in. x 53 in.
Photo by Victor Monsour

BRINDAN BYRNE, MICHAEL
SIM and JOAN IRVING
La Jolla, Calif.

"Seat du Verre" (Seat of Glass)
Ebonized white oak,
macassar ebony
24 in. x 20 in. x 44 in.
Photo by Alan Watson

KIMBERLY A. KELZER
Oakland, Calif.

"Cowch"
Ebonized cherry,
calfskin, stainless steel
58 in. x 28 in. x 39 in.
Photo by Kimberly A. Kelzer

27

MICHAEL McALEENAN
Gloucester, Mass.

"In Celebration of Tulips"
Black walnut
42 in. x 20 in. x 20 in.
Photo by Lance Patterson

DANIEL PECK
San Antonio, Tex.

Settee
Mahogany, wenge;
original art on aluminum
panels by Harold J. Wood
61 in. x 33 in. x 29 in.
Photo by Swain Eden

REBECCA HEIL
Ellensburg, Wash.

Weaving bench
Curly red oak
32 in. x 16 in. x 26 in.
Photo by Mark Sexton

MICHAEL A. GREGORIO
Oceanside, N.Y.

Rocking chair
Mahogany
46 in. x 27 in. x 45 in.
Photo by Bruce Morgan

JAEGER & ERNST, INC.
Barboursville, Va.

"Kelley Chair"
Koa
18 in. x 19 in. x 38 in.
Photo by Philip Beaurline

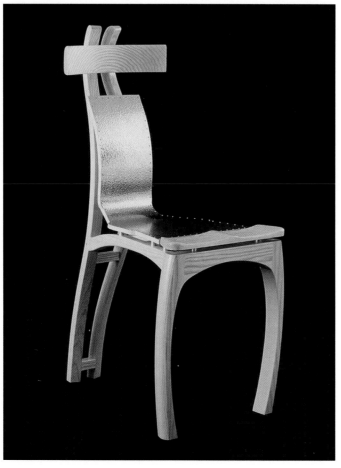

JIM HOLAHAN
Lansing, N.Y.

Pull-up chair
Ash, poplar, stainless steel
21 in. x 17 in. x 34 in.
Photo by Jim Holahan

STEVE STENSTROM
Boston, Mass.

Chippendale arm chair
Cherry
28¾ in. x 23 in. x 40½ in.
Photo by Lance Patterson

HERBERT A. HAESSLER
Lincoln, Mass.

Valet chair
Red oak, teak
19 in. x 18 in. x 35 in.
Photo by Talbot D. Lovering

JOHN HURDEL
Des Moines, Iowa

"Empress Josephine"
Maple, ebony, leather
16½ in. x 18½ in. x 27½ in.
Photo by Pete Krumhardt

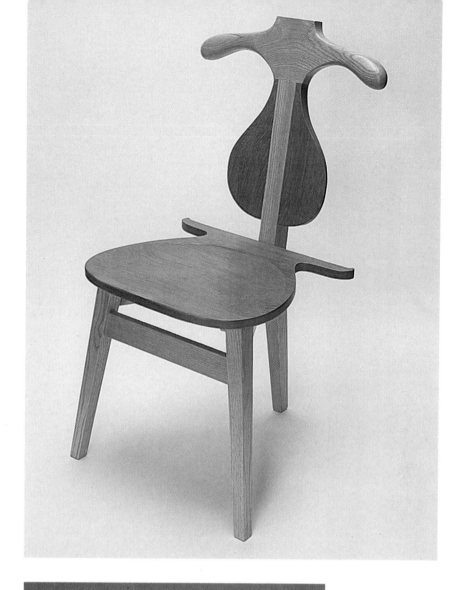

JAMES B. SAGUI
Boston, Mass.

High-back chair
Curly maple and ebony
18 in. x 16 in. x 55 in.
Photo by David du Busc

JOHN BLAZY
Hiram, Ohio

"The Orient Goes Modern"
Ebonized oak
59 in. x 18 in. x 17 in.
Photo by John Blazy

MARK SFIRRI and
ROBERT DODGE
New Hope, Pa.

"Chair of Elijah"
Lacewood, acrylic, gold leaf
14 in. x 14 in. x 34 in.
Photo by Mark Sfirri

DAVID CRAMER
West Redding, Conn.

"Crypto-Egypto Neo-Nouveau
Blub Blub Chippendale Chair"
Honduras mahogany
20 in. x 27 in. x 37 in.
Photo by Kevin McDonald

DAVID CRAMER
West Redding, Conn.

"Oceania Bench"
Honduras mahogany, ebonized
mahogany, basswood
24 in. x 51 in. x 48 in.
Photo by Kevin McDonald

STEVE BROWN
Ipswich, Mass.

Heart-back side chair
Mahogany
20 in. x 20 in. x 38 in.
Photo by Lance Patterson

RAY KELSO
TREEBEARD DESIGNS, INC.
Collegeville, Pa.

Rocking chair
Walnut, cherry
28 in. x 47 in. x 48 in.
Photo by Tom Crane Photography

STEPHEN PERRIN
Timonium, Md.

"Empire"
Rocking chair
Maple
31 in. x 23 in. x 50 in.
Photo by David Simpson

JAN OLEWNIK
Manhattan, Kans.

Love seat
Ash
62 in. x 28 in. x 42 in.
Photo by Rod Mikinski

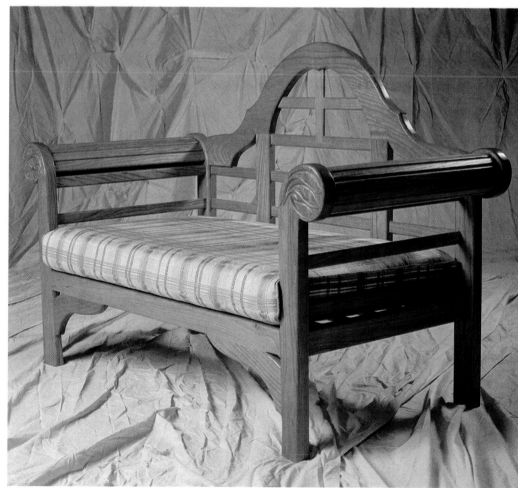

CURTIS BUCHANAN
Jonesborough, Tenn.

High chair
Sugar maple, pine, red oak
11½ in. x 17 in. x 37½ in.
Photo by Tom Pardue

JONATHAN PRESSLER
Rochester, N.Y.

Chair
Maple, tiger maple
19 in. x 21 in. x 31 in.
Photo by Tony Gerardi

DENNIS R. LOVELAND
Portland, Ore.

"Tuxedo Chair"
Bird's-eye maple,
ebonized maple
22 in. x 20 in. x 40 in.
Photo by Mike Patterson

JAMIE ROBERTSON
W. Concord, Mass.

"Water Bench"
Lemonwood,
East Indian rosewood
58 in. x 16 in. x 27 in.
Photo by Dean Powell

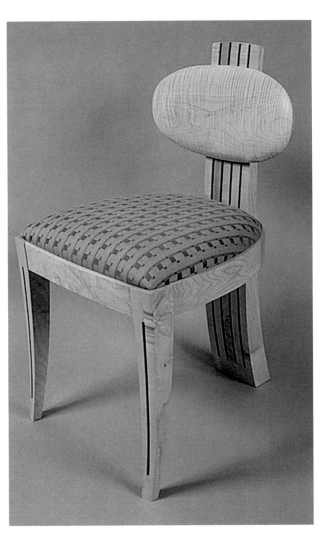

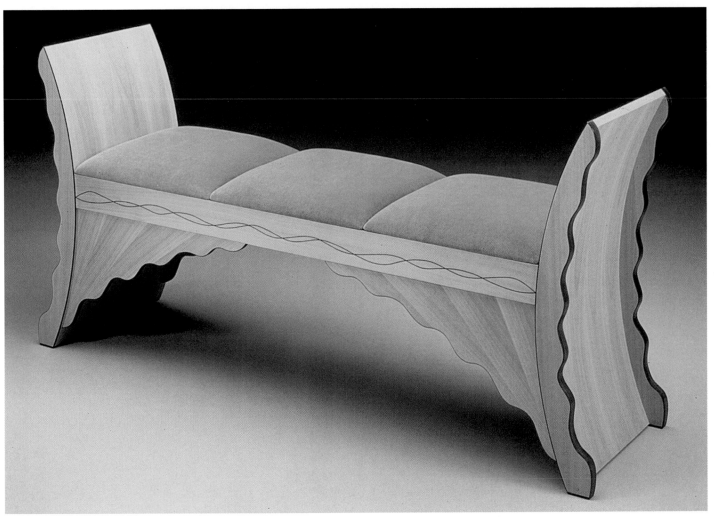

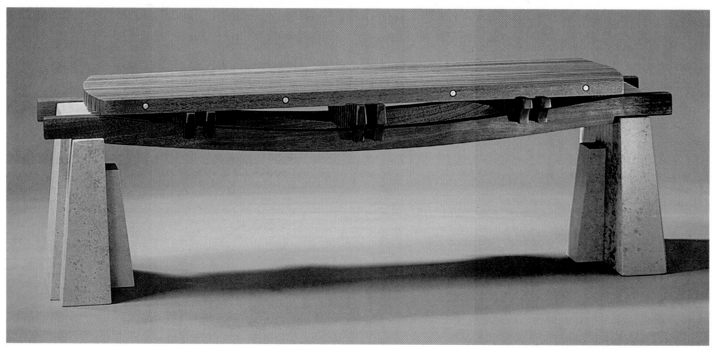

JACK HARICH
Atlanta, Ga.

Shell-back rocker and
rocking ottoman
Curly maple, walnut
45 in. x 29 in. x 45 in.
Photo by Kevin Rose

GREGG R. LIPTON
Cumberland, Maine

Rocking chair
Cherry
44 in. x 23 in. x 42 in.
Photo by Warren Roos

DON TREDINNICK
Greensboro, N.C.

Hall chair
Curly maple
18½ in. x 17½ in. x 51 in.
Photo by Paul Dodge

DAN KAGAY
Florence, Tex.

"Akhenaton's Bench"
Honduras mahogany, aluminum,
copper, limestone
66 in. x 16 in. x 18 in.
Photo by Ron Whitfield

VIRGINIA B. GLENNON
Boston, Mass.

"Notmygrandmother's
Hall Settle"
Ash, white oak
56 in. x 18½ in. x 72 in
Photo by Lance Patterson

Tables

LOY DAVIS MARTIN
Palo Alto, Calif.

Occasional table
Masur birch, holly, willow, East
Indian laurel, ebony
23 in. x 20½-in. dia.
Photo by Paul Fairchild

BARRY T. MACDONALD
Grosse Pointe, Mich.

Foyer table
Mahogany crotch veneer,
mahogany, walnut
30 in. x 48-in. dia.
Photo by Barry T. Macdonald

MARK D. BELANGER
Tewksbury, Mass.

New York card table
Mahogany
34 in. x 16 in. x 26 in.
Photo by Lance Patterson

ANDREW JACOBSON
Petaluma, Calif.

Entry table
Macassar ebony, abracia ,
nouvelle marble, 24k gold leaf
74 in. x 16 in. x 32 in.
Photo by D. Anderson Photo

CARLTON B. CRAIG
Bassett, Va.

18th-century card table
Mahogany, hard maple,
crotch mahogany
33 in. x 16½ in. x 29¾ in. (closed)
33 in. x 33 in. x 29¾ in. (open)
Photo by Mike Arnold

LEO SADLEK
Neerim South, Victoria,
Australia

Table
Australian ash, black lacquer
New Guinea walnut
28 in. x 22-in. dia.
Photo by Straight Photography

JONATHAN WRIGHT
Jamaica Plain, Mass.

Extension dining table
Fiddleback mahogany,
curly sycamore
29½ in. x 52-in. dia.
Photo by Dean Powell

STEPHEN PERRIN
Timonium, Md.

"Chaps"
End table
Cherry lacewood, padauk
23 in. x 20 in. x 22 in.
Photo by Even Cohen

GLENN WARD
Oakville, Ontario, Canada

"Semion"
Curly sycamore,
purpleheart, ash
54 in. x 18 in. x 36 in.
Photo by Glenn Ward

GLENN MILLER
Ludlowville, N.Y.

Coffee table
Cherry
60 in. x 24 in. x 20 in.
Photo by Bill Faley

JOHN GOFF
San Diego, Calif.

Newport-style game table
Mahogany, tulip poplar
34 in. x 17 in. x 27 in.
Photo by Joe Klien

THOMAS HUGH STANGELAND
Seattle, Wash.

Sitting-room table
Cherry, ebony
50 in. x 18 in. x 24 in.
Photo by Chris Barth

MARC A. ADAMS
Franklin, Ind.

"Hershey Table"
Curly English sycamore,
miscellaneous veneers
38 in. x 20 in. x 33½ in.
Photo by Gary Chilluffo

JANE GREENBERG
Boston, Mass.

Coffee table
Padauk, maple
35 in. x 40½ in. x 15½ in.
Photo by Dean Powell

CARL TESE
Brooklyn, N.Y.

"Birth of Venus"
Curly maple, anegre, ebony,
peacock feathers
30 in. x 16 in. x 31 in.
Photo by Marcus Tullis

51

TERRY H. ANDERSON
Portland, Ore.

"Reptable"
Lacewood, rosewood,
Baltic-birch plywood,
copper, leather
64 in. x 39 in. x 18 in.
Photo by Edward Gowans

RICK NORRANDER
Portland, Ore.

"Time to Fly"
Walnut, maple inlay
40 in. x 17 in. x 17 in.
Photo by Studio 3, Inc.

JAMIE ROBERTSON
West Concord, Mass.

Gaming table
East Indian rosewood,
pau amarello
29 in. x 52-in. dia.
Photo by Dean Powell

KIM SCHMAHMANN
Cambridge, Mass.

Manhattan coffee table
Mahogany, birch, ash
36 in. x 36 in. x 17 in.
Photo by Lance Patterson

BRIAN TINIUS
N. Hollywood, Calif.

Coffee table
Poplar, padauk, wenge inlay
54 in. x 24 in. x 14 in.
Photo by Brian Tinius

LANCE PATTERSON
Boston, Mass.

Pembroke tables
Mahogany, holly inlay
30 in. x 18 in. x 28 in. (closed)
30 in. x 36½ in. x 28 in. (open)
Photo by Lance Patterson

AL MILLER
Portland, Ore.

Twisted table
Ash
18 in. x 12 in. x 45 in.
Photo by David Browne

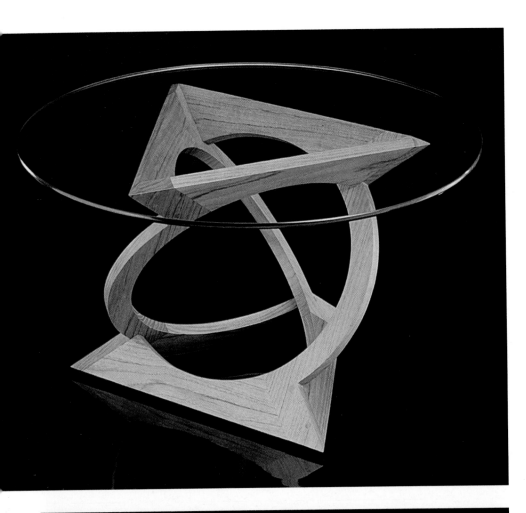

DUANE CLARK
Falls Church, Va.

Coffee table
Teak
17 in. x 30-in. dia.
Photo by John Barber

GREGORY W. GUENTHER
Savannah, Ga.

"Tilt Top Twosome"
Zebra wood, ebony
14½ in. x 25½ in. x 18¼-in. dia.
Photo by Tim Rhoad and Associates

SUSAN PFEIFFER
Elizabethtown, Ky.

"Petroleum Invasion"
(Detail above right)
Ebonized cherry, basswood,
neon and argon lights
42 in. x 42 in. x 18 in.
Photo by Scott Mitchell

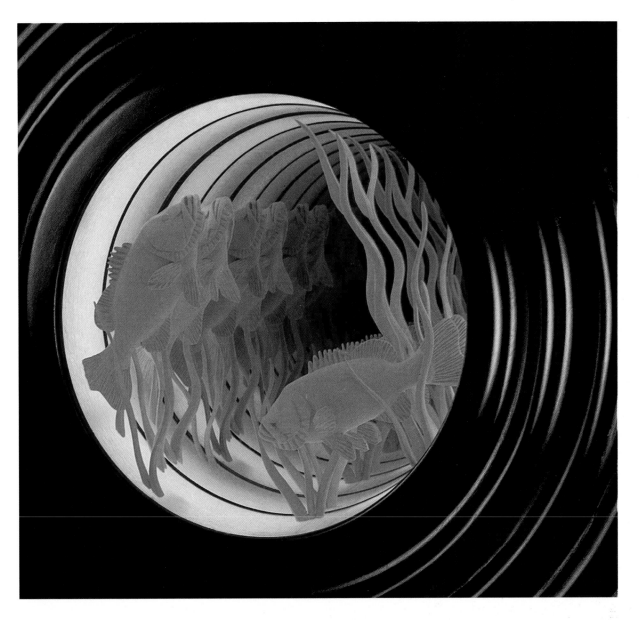

JERRY ALONZO
Geneseo, N.Y.

Hall table with mirror
Cherry, maple
Table: 36 in. x 16 in. x 34 in.
Mirror: 18 in. x 36 in.
Photo by Ron Pretzer

DALE BROHOLM
Wellesley, Mass.

Double-gate-leg table
Teak, ebony, madrone-burl
veneer, plywood, epoxy resin
56 in. x 56 in. x 28 in.
Photo by Dean Powell

GARY ROGOWSKI
Portland, Ore.

"Dancing on Thin Ice II"
Maple, medium-density
fiberboard, black
lacquer, rosewood
43 in. x 20 in. x 17 in.
Photo by Harold Wood

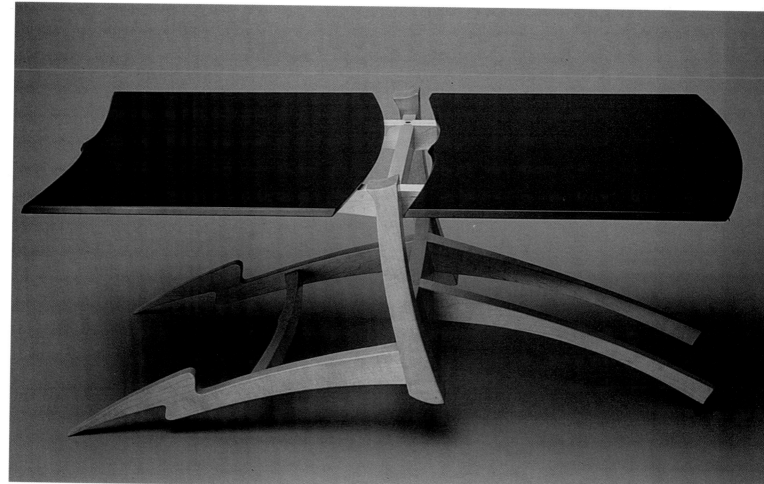

SIMON IVES
Toronto, Ontario, Canada

Entrance hall table
Ash, stained maple
40 in. x 12 in. x 33 in.
Photo by Simon Ives

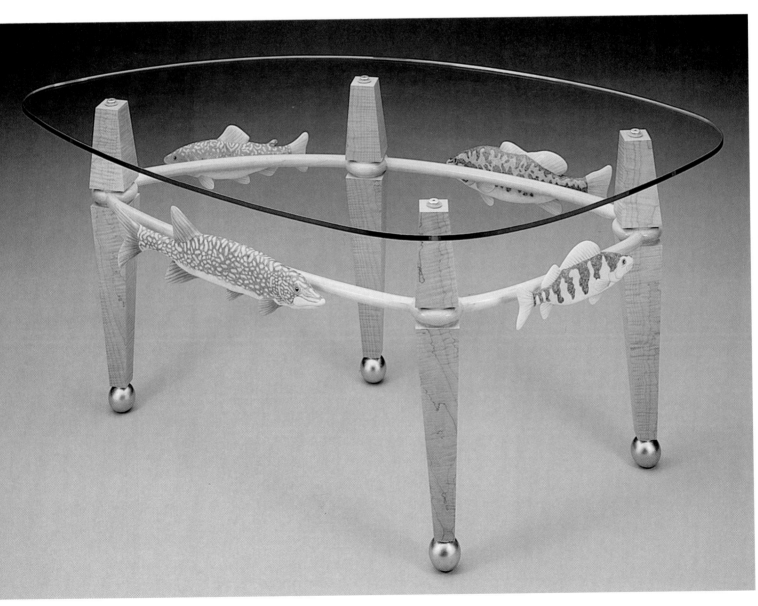

ROBERT A. SPANGLER
Seattle, Wash.

"Krake Table"
(Detail above)
Mahogany, curly birch,
fir, ebony
36 in. x 15 in. x 29 in.
Photo by Mel Curtis

JOEL EVETT and
ROBERTA BOYLEN
Belmont, Mass.

"Fish Table"
Tiger maple, poplar, gesso,
egg tempera, gold leaf, glass
50 in. x 30 in. x 22 in.
Photo by A. Dean Powell

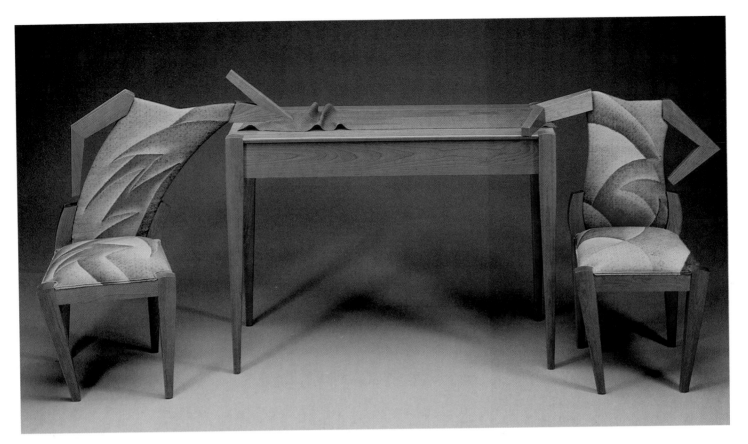

GREGORY W. GUENTHER
Savannah, Ga.

Hepplewhite card table
Mahogany, madrone burl,
ebony, rosewood, maple
36 in. x 18 in. x 29½ in.
Photo by Tim Rhoad
and Associates

RIC WILEY
San Diego, Calif.

Side table
Mahogany
59½ in. x 16½ in. x 28¾ in.
Photo by Rich Ford

RICHARD L. FORD, JR.
San Diego, Calif.

"Hal & Stewart"
Cherry, silk
96 in. x 22 in. x 41 in.
Photo by Dean Powell

A. SCOTT MACFARLANE
Denver, Colo.

Hall table
Bird's-eye maple,
bloodwood, cocobolo
36 in. x 15 in. x 36 in.
Photo by Tim Loomis

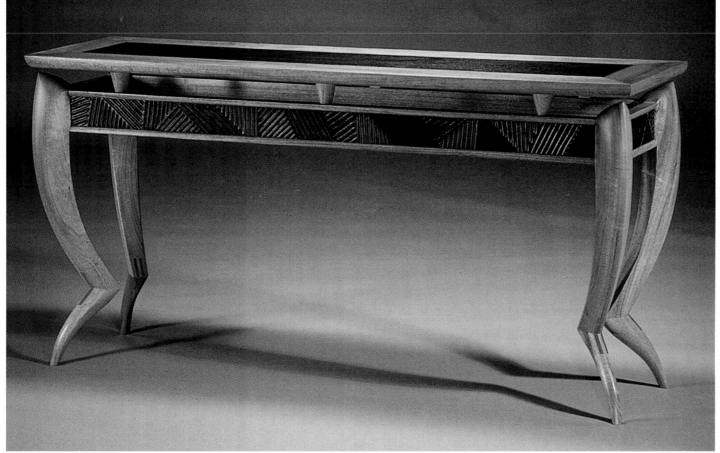

MIKE FLANAGAN
Petaluma, Calif.

Table
Lacewood, cocobolo
24 in. x 18-in. dia.
Photo by Steven Mette

PAUL KOENIG
Traverse City, Mich.

Federal-style card table
Mahogany, aspen, bubinga,
holly, ebony
35 in. x 17½ in. x 30 in. (closed)
35 in. x 35 in. x 30 in. (open)
Photo by Lance Patterson

ROGER CHARLES SHERRY
Staten Island, N.Y.

"Magnum in the Corner Pocket"
Sapele pommelle, purpleheart,
bronze, copper, chrome, lacquer
108 in. x 45 in. x 30 in.
Photo by Mike Pencak

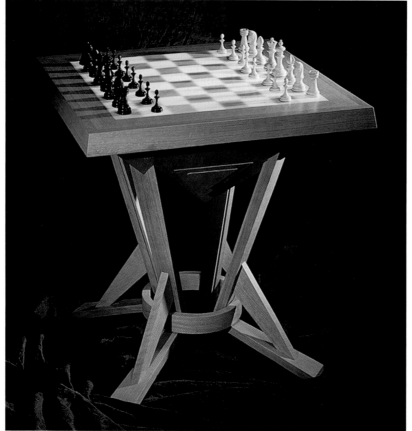

KENTON T. RUSE
Topeka, Kans.

Lighted chess table
White oak, Corian
24 in. x 24 in. x 26 in.
Photo by Nathan Ham
Photography

DAVID ORTH
Oak Park, Ill.

Triangle coffee table
Ebonized anegre, red oak
48 in. x 32 in. x 15 in.
Photo by Aldis Darre

JOHN DUNSTAN
Clayburn, B.C., Canada

"Octovolo"
Pedestal table
Quilted maple, bird's-eye maple
66 in. x 39 in. x 30 in.
Photo by Andrew W. Simpson

JAMES BACIGALUPI
San Jose, Calif.

"Twig Under Zorro's Cape"
Walnut, poplar, glass, lacquer
36 in. x 18 in. x 22 in.
Photo by Dennis Anderson

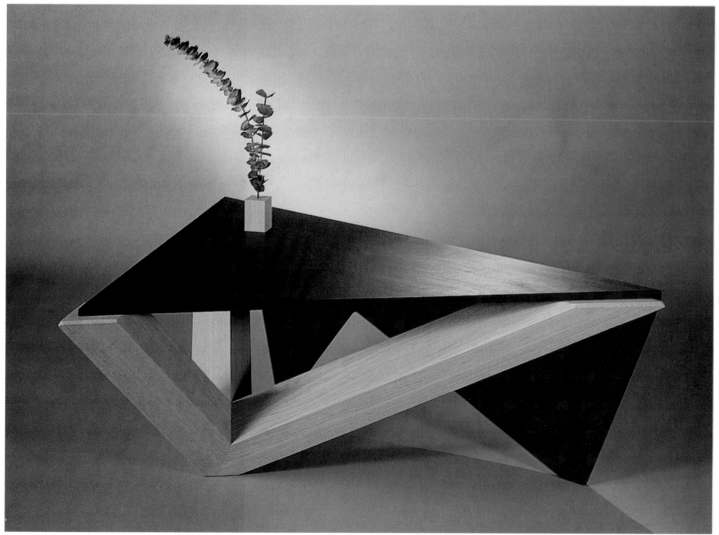

Boxes & Chests

GLEN G. GRANT
Andover, Mass.

"A Night on the Town"
South American mahogany,
black walnut
38 in. x 20 in. x 72 in.
Photo by Spectrum Photo

TOMMY R. BROWN
Richmond, Ky.

Sunburst keepsake chest
Cherry, walnut burl
21 in. x 11½ in. x 8½ in.
Photo by Kara Beth Brunner

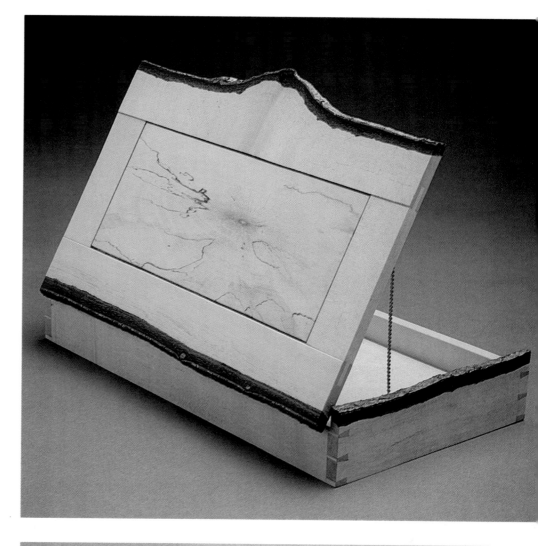

ROGER GIFKINS
Kempsey, New South Wales,
Australia

Bark-edged jewelry box
Beach acronychia
11 in. x 7 in. x 1½ in.
Photo by George Seras

GEORGE LEVIN
Seattle, Wash.

Jewelry box
Cherry, ebony
8½ in. x 5¼ in. x 3⅝ in.
Photo by George Levin

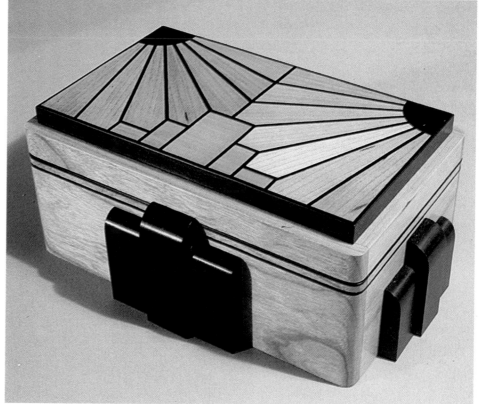

MARK NATHENSON
Rochester, N.Y.

Southwest blanket chest
Purpleheart, curly maple,
poplar, mother-of-pearl,
faux turquoise
52 in. x 28 in. x 27 in.
Photo by Hampton Bridwell

MICHAEL ELKAN
Silverton, Ore.

"Path to the Falls"
Nested boxes
Redwood burl
8 in. x 10 in. x 26 in.
Photo by Eric Griswold

DINO MATTIOLI
St. Helena, Calif.

Tansu sea chest
Oak, mahogany
20 in. x 20 in. x 21 in.
Photo by Steven Zanelli

MICHAEL HAMILTON
Boise, Idaho

"Double Decker Box"
Bubinga, bloodwood,
ebony, maple, brass
11 in. x 7 in. x 8 in.
Photo by George Post

STACEY SMITH
Rochester, N.Y.

Silver chest
Mahogany
36 in. x 18 in. x 44 in.
Photo by Hussey
Photographic Arts

MICHAEL SNOW JONES
and BO ESREY
Mount Gretna, Pa.

Jewelry cabinet
Bloodwood, purpleheart,
walnut, birch
18 in. x 12 in. x 12 in.
Photo by Art Clagett/Photography
by Simone

JOHN FISCHER
Brooklyn, N.Y.

Tool chest
Curly maple, mahogany,
ash, poplar
34 in. x 17¾ in. x 20¾ in.
Photo by Lance Patterson

JIM McCANN
Trotwood, Ohio

Jewelry/lingerie chest
Honduras mahogany, curly
maple, hard maple,
black velvet
16 in. x 16 in. x 42¾ in.
Photo by Daniel F. Gabriel
Photography

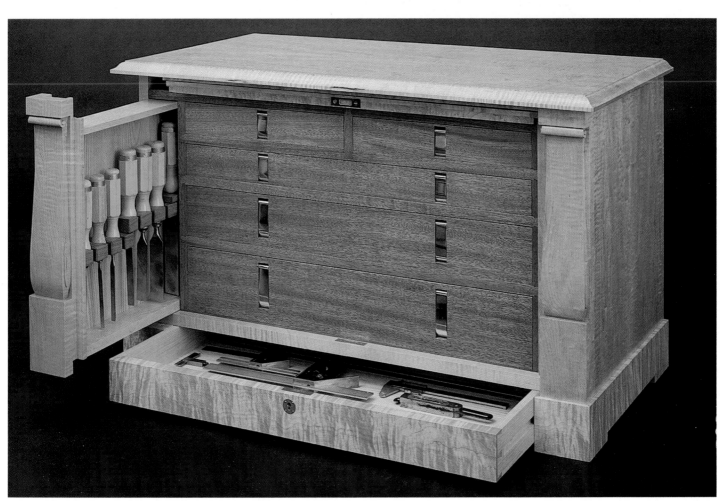

RAY JONES
Asheville, N.C.

"Hidden Treasure"
Baltic-birch plywood,
ebony, padauk
7¼ in. x 10-in. dia.
Photo by John Warner

RACHEL PAXTON and
ERIC SWANSON
Jamaica Plain, Mass.

Chest over drawers
Rock maple, cedar, ebony,
oxidized brass, paint
38 in. x 17 in. x 28 in.
Photo by Pat Cudahy

JAMES CASEBOLT
Santa Cruz, Calif.

Table chest
Red elm, black walnut
44 in. x 20 in. x 20 in.
Photo by Daniel Quijano

THOMAS J. MONAHAN
Cedar Rapids, Iowa

Jewelry box
Purpleheart, aluminum,
polyester
22 in. x 11 in. x 6 in.
Photo by Peter Krumhardt

DINO MATTIOLI
St. Helena, Calif.

Tansu step-style chest
Pine, purpleheart
41 in. x 12 in. x 41 in.
Photo by Steven Zanelli

DAVID H. MEIKLEM
Yantic, Conn.

Lingerie cabinet
Black walnut, bird's-eye maple
24 in. x 17 in. x 54 in.
Photo by Pietro

ROWEN JORDAN CAPLAN
Plainfield, Mass.

Tool chest
Ash, bubinga, ebony
21½ in. x 10 in. x 13½ in.
Photo by Arthur Evans
Photographer

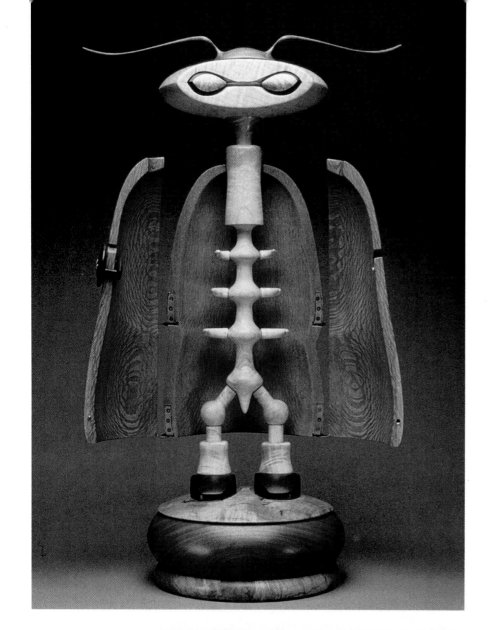

MICHAEL J. BROLLY
Hamburg, Pa.

"Self-Portrait of the Artist
as a Young Man"
Jewelry box
Lacewood, mahogany, maple,
purpleheart, bubinga, ebony,
varigated gold leaf
27 in. x 10-in. dia.
Photo by David Haas

THOMAS H. DONETH
Wasilla, Alaska

Jewelry chests
Cherry, walnut, white oak,
red oak, Baltic-birch plywood
10 in. x 6 in. x 23 in.
Photo by Greg Martin

ROBERT E. MARCH
Princeton, Mass.

Lidded container
Pear, maple
5 in. x 9½ in. x 20 in.
Photo by Frank Martin

STEPHEN R. ALEXANDER
Baltimore, Md.

"North Bennet
Street School Box"
Poplar, oak, mahogany
32 in. x 19 in. x 17 in.
Photo by Lance Patterson

Desks

DAVID GRAY
Freeland, Wash.

Scallop-shell desk
Honduras mahogany,
walnut, ebony
42 in. x 42 in. x 35 in.
Photo by Gregg Krogstadd

STEPHEN DANIELL
Easthampton, Mass.

Elliptical escritoire
and Ginkgo chair
Bird's-eye maple, painted
cherry, black inlay
Desk: 46 in. x 28 in. x 30 in.
Chair: 19 in. x 23 in. x 34 in.
Photo by Michael Latil

SLAV YELESIJEVICH
Chicago, Ill.

Artist's workstation
Maple, padauk,
ebony, lemonwood,
African satinwood
72 in. x 36 in. x 32 in.
Photo by Kevin Downey

BRETON FLANNERY WOODWORKS
Freeport, Maine

Woman's curved writing desk
Washed cherry, acrylic paints
60 in. x 30 in. x 30 in.
Photo by John Tanabe

KELLY MEHLER
Berea, Ky.

Federal secretary
Mahogany, quilted maple,
satinwood, ebony, holly
37 in. x 21 in. x 74 in.
Photo by Albert Mooney

ALAN McMASTER
Brighton, Mich.

Desk and credenza
Red oak, purpleheart
Desk: 96 in. x 42 in. x 30 in.
Credenza: 204 in. x 24 in. x 30 in.
Photo by Rob Van Marter

WYATT RENK
Point Reyes Station, Calif.

Percell desk
Goncalo alves, macassar
ebony, pau amarello
60 in. x 22 in. x 29½ in.
Photo by Art Rogers

GEORGE LEVIN
Seattle, Wash.

Federal-period desk
Mahogany, holly, ebony
42 in. x 21½ in. x 45 in.
Photo by John Black

TERRY MOORE
Newport, N.H.

Lady's writing desk
Bubinga, curly maple
54 in. x 24 in. x 30 in.
Photo by Thomas Ames, Jr.

DOUGLAS SIGLER
Penland, N.C.

Dressing table and stool
Maple, mahogany,
black lacquer, Corian
49 in. x 24 in. x 29 in.
Photo by Barts Art

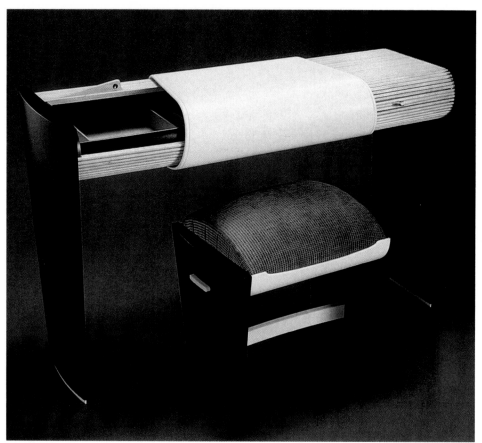

RONALD C. BERGENHEIM
Boston, Mass.

Desk
Mahogany, mahogany
"pudding" veneer, holly,
ebony, leather
53 in. x 25½ in. x 30 in.
Photo by Lance Patterson

BRAD E. SCHWARTZ
Deer Isle, Maine

Desk and chair
Pecan, cocobolo
44 in. x 19¼ in. x 29 in.
Photo by David Klopfenstein

PETER NARAMORE
Kula, Hawaii

Desk
White maple, fossilized marble
62 in. x 36 in. x 30 in.
Photo by Steve Minkowski

ROBERT S. OGILVIE
Nashville, Tenn.

Desk
Maple, curly maple
72 in. x 36 in. x 30½ in.
Photo by Bob Hoffman

ERIC NEIL ROTH
San Diego, Calif.

"Eraser Head"
Drafting table
Poplar, lauan mahogany,
alder, ash
48 in. x 33 in. x 29 in.
Photo by Kim Kelzer

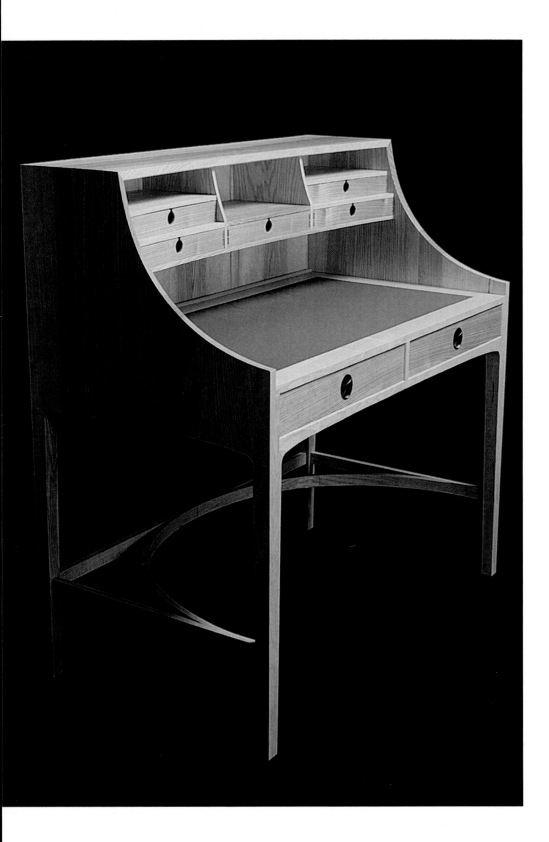

RAY KELSO and RODGER BLYE
TREEBEARD DESIGNS, INC.
Collegeville, Pa.

Desk
Walnut, cherry
63 in. x 45 in. x 30 in.
Photo by Tom Crane Photography

GLENN HUGHES
Revere, Pa.

"School of Sharks"
Lacewood, curly sycamore
60 in. x 30 in. x 30 in.
Photo by Mitch Mandel

VIC MATTHEWS
Coromandel, New Zealand

Writing desk
New Zealand ash, leather
43½ in. x 24 in. x 43½ in.
Photo by Eric Lens

DAVID GREGSON
Burston, Norfolk, England

Bureau and chair
Olive ash, brown oak,
cedar of Lebanon, ebony
36½ in. x 27½ in. x 54 in.
Photo by David Gregson

ROGER HEITZMAN
Scotts Valley, Calif.

Desk
Curly maple
48 in. x 24 in. x 46 in.
Photo by Roger Heitzman

Beds & Furnishings

*MARK DALE SMITH
and RENEE A. HILL.
New Meadows, Idaho*

"Wildwood Tree"
Idaho yellow pine
96 in. x 84 in. x 144 in.
Photo by Steve Welsh

MARK SFIRRI and ROBERT DODGE
New Hope, Pa.

Folding screen
Mahogany, gold leaf, acrylic
48 in. x 2 in. x 84 in.
Photo by David Graham

RALF KEELER
Seattle, Wash.

Bed
Padauk, curly western maple
80 in. x 60 in. x 36 in.
Photo by Stan Shockey

STEPHEN TURINO
Wakefield, R.I.

Queen-size bed and
bedside chests
Lacewood, macassar ebony,
Gaboon ebony
Bed: 86 in. x 65 in. x 44 in.
Chests: 18 in. x 18 in. x 26 in.
Photo by Ric Murray

STEPHEN TRUSLOW
New York, N.Y.

Three-quarter-round library
Curly maple, purpleheart,
ebony veneers
93 in. x 150-in. dia.
Photo by Jonathan Wallen

DAVID VALCOVIC
Salem, Mass.

Room-divider screen
Mahogany, silk, copper
68 in. x 1¾ in. x 75 in.
Photo by Rob Huntley

CRAFT-WOOD PRODUCTS
Andover, Mass.
Carved bed
South American mahogany,
black walnut
80 in. x 76 in. x 52 in.
Photo by Spectrum Photo

KIRK von KUNDTZ
Cleveland Heights, Ohio

Bed
Quilted maple,
bird's-eye maple
84 in. x 90 in. x 72 in.
Photo by Andrew Gordon

JOHN SCHWARZTKOPF
Cedar Rapids, Iowa

Folding screens
White oak,
Honduras mahogany
112 in. x 1½ in. x 84 in.
Photo by Rod Bradley

COLLINS CARPENTER
Canandaigua, N.Y.

Cradle
Red oak
44 in. x 26 in. x 48 in.
Photo by Michael Mink

CRAIG WOODWARD
Spring Valley, Calif.

Queen-size bed
Figured avodire, padauk,
ash, black lacquer
108 in. x 84 in. x 84 in.
Photo by Jon Woodward

DENIS J. SEMPREBON, STEVE
NYSTROM and WILL NEPTUNE
Stow, Mass.

Traditional mantelpiece
(Detail above)
South American mahogany
86 in. x 11¾ in. x 54 in.
Photo by Lance Patterson

DUANE BROWN
San Diego, Calif.

Door
Philippine mahogany
80 in. x 36 in.
Photo by Victor Brown

WENDOVER WOODWORKS
Newburyport, Mass.

Queen-size bed
Mahogany, curly maple, ebony
82 in. x 62 in. x 42 in.
Photo by Bill Truslow

JOHN DODD
Rochester, N.Y.

Screen/room divider with
display cabinet
Anegre, cherry, wenge
36 in. x 16 in. x 84 in.
Photo by Woody Packard

JEFFREY GREENE
New Hope, Pa.

Carved cradle
Black walnut
38 in. x 16 in. x 15 in.
Photo by Randyl Bye

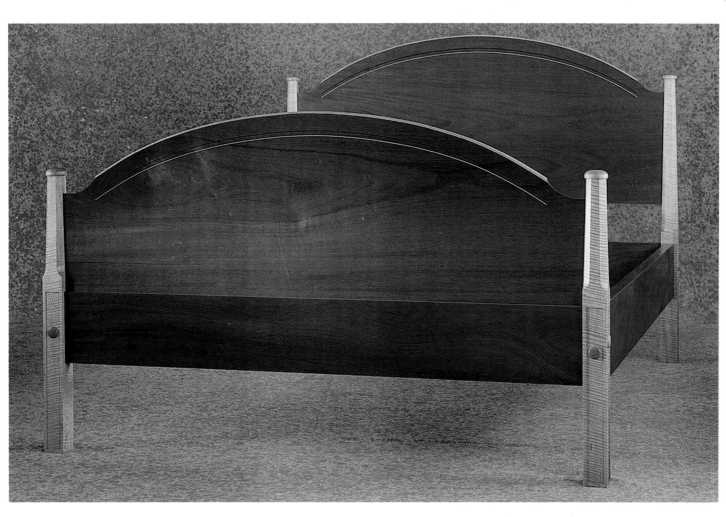

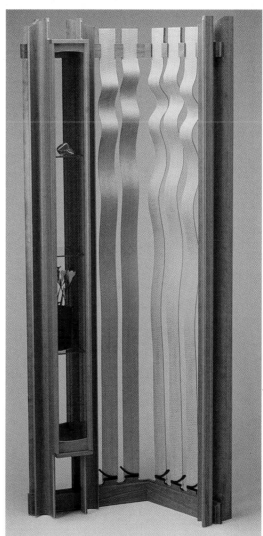

WILLIAM J. SCHNUTE
Carmel Valley, Calif.

Entry doors
(Detail below)
White oak
108 in. x 9 in. x 84 in.
Photo by Tom O'Neal

MARK BIRMINGHAM
Fort Collins, Colo.

Raised-panel four-poster bed
Walnut, pecan, honey locust
96 in. x 72 in. x 36 in.
Photo by Jim Cambon

OSWALD MARTIN
Chicago, Ill.

Hand-carved king-size bed
Mahogany, lacquer
81 in. x 78 in. x 24 in.
Photo by Ky Boe

LEO SADLEK
Neerim South, Victoria,
Australia

Bed
Silky oak, stained coachwood,
rose shea oak
84 in. x 72 in. x 36 in.
Photo by Straight Photography

O'NEAL JONES
Graham, N.C.

Three-panel *shoji* screen
Ash, walnut, fiberglass
72 in. x 90 in.
Photo by Diane Davis

JOHN ARENSKOV
Mira Loma, Calif.

Console bed
Bubinga, wenge
108 in. x 168 in. x 57 in.
Photo by Deborah Ford

Sculpture & Carvings

ARNOLD R. ALTSHULER
Bethesda, Md.

"Puff the Dragon"
Baltic birch, padauk, cherry
40 in. x 14 in. x 48 in.
Photo by William Schaeffer

MILES LUND
Boise, Idaho

Pine-tree western boots
and box
Ponderosa pine
Box: 17¼ in. x 14 in. x 5¼ in.
Boots: 12 in. x 4¼ in. x 14⅜ in.
Photo by Bob Richey

ROBERT E. FOJUT
Greendale, Wis.

"Detective Truman Strong"
Basswood
5 in. x 10 in. x 12 in.
Photo by Jim Wend

FRED COGELOW
Willmar, Minn.

"Another Beer at Rosie's"
Butternut
23½ in. x 5¼ in. x 22 in.
Photo by Robert Mischka

JOHN C. SHARP
Mineral Point, Wis.

"Wreck About to Happen"
Black walnut
33 in. x 20 in. x 25 in.
Photo by Bill Lemke

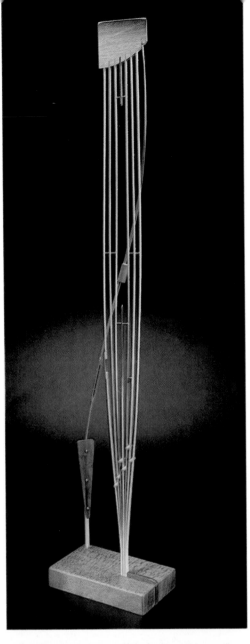

NIALL F. BARRETT
Narrowsburg, N.Y.

"Macy's Windows"
(Far left)
Lacewood, poplar, padauk
6 in. x 10½ in. x 50 in.
Photo by Chris Holden

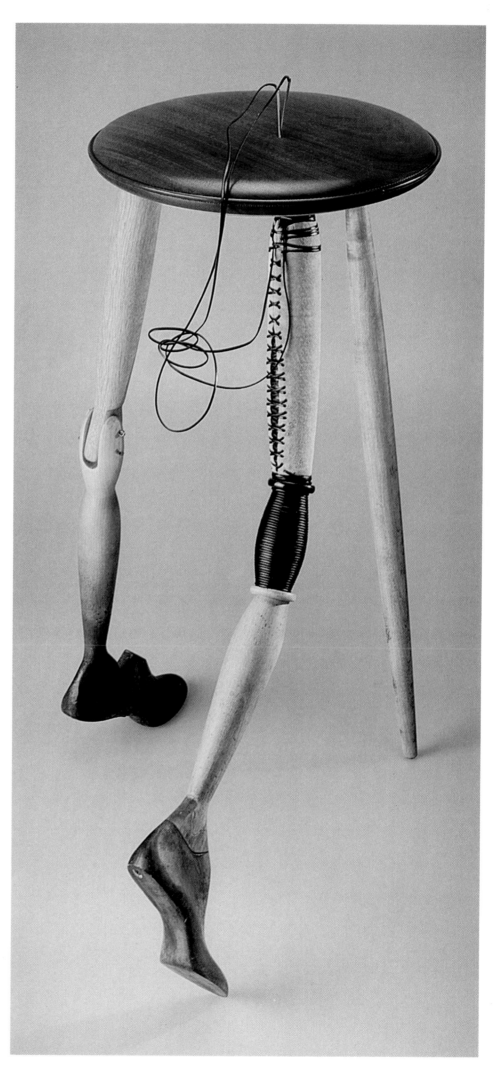

LOGAN FRY
Richfield, Ohio

"Post-Modern Hippoglyphics"
Ash, locust, plywood
26 in. x 20 in. x 60 in.
Photo by Jean Schnell

ROBERT GETZEN
Hana, Hawaii

"Kahiko"
Wall hanging
Mango, black monkey pod,
mamee apple, koa,
pheasantwood, milo
42 in. x 2½ in. x 20 in.
Photo by Rob Ratkowski

NEIL J. DONOVAN
Erie, Pa.

"Walking Stool"
Honduras mahogany,
maple, oak, cherry, leather lace
20 in. x 14 in. x 30 in.
Photo by Mark and Debra Fainstein

WILLIAM J. SCHNUTE
Carmel Valley, Calif.

Above-mantel carving
White oak, stone
168 in. x 8 in. x 114 in.
Photo by Tom O'Neal

NORSK WOOD WORKS, LTD.
Barronett, Wis.

Split-tail ale bowl
Basswood
16 in. x 6¾ in. x 6¾ in.
Photo by Robert Mischka

*MARK DALE SMITH
and RENEE A. HILL
New Meadows, Idaho*

"Anaconda and Orchids"
Idaho yellow pine,
maple, black willow
54 in. x 96 in.
Photo by Steve Welsh

NEIL COX
Ingersoll, Ontario, Canada

"Saint Alexis"
Butternut
17 in. x 15 in. x 44 in.
Photo by Robert Mischka

CHARLES FORSTER
Portland, Ore.

"Etheria"
Walnut, apple
18 in. x 12 in. x 29 in.
Photo by Harold Wood

RON RAMSEY
Nevada City, Calif.

"Under Water"
Butternut
35 in. x 8 in. x 25 in.
Photo by Richard Sargent

RAY WINDER
Merstham, Surrey, England

Acorns
English oak, limewood
16 in. x 11 in. x 3 in.
Photo by Ray Winder

JOHN C. SHARP
Mineral Point, Wis.

"Wahktageli, Yankton Sioux"
Black walnut, black lacquer
12 in. x 15 in. x 26 in.
Photo by Bill Lemke

CHUCK ENGBERG
Alameda, Calif.

Black duck decoy
Basswood
16 in. x 5½ in. x 5 in.
Photo by Chuck Engberg

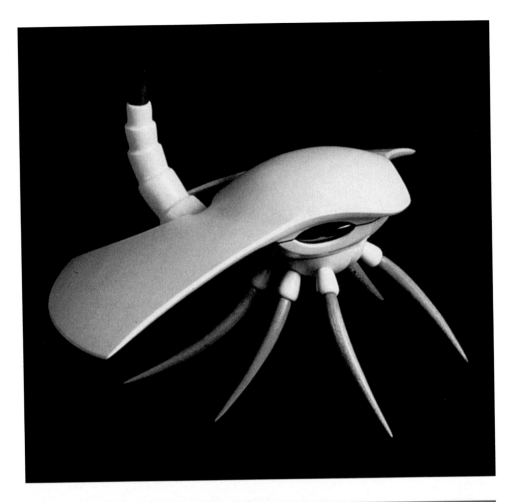

MICHAEL J. BROLLY
Hamburg, Pa.

"Moth"
Holly, cherry, ebony
10 in. x 11 in. x 6 in.
Photo by Michael J. Brolly

JOHN CONARD
El Cajon, Calif.

"Arthur"
Carousel horse
Poplar
50 in. x 11 in. x 42 in.
Photo by Denise Tondreau

DANIEL KREIMER
Cincinnati, Ohio

Angel pull toy
Birch
10 in. x 5 in. x 10 in.
Photo by Caleb Faux

Turnings

JOHN JORDAN
Antioch, Tenn.

Textured jar
Box elder, pink ivory
11 in. x 9-in. dia.
Photo by John S. Cummings

DENNIS R. LOVELAND
Portland, Ore.

"Spider"
Ebony, holly
3 in. x 9-in. dia.
Photo by Mike Patterson

BRENDA BEHRENS
Pomona, Calif.

"Enclosed Form #80102"
Purpleheart, maple, black
walnut, oak, padauk
2¾ in. x 9-in. dia.
Photo by Tom Griffin

NEIL J. DONOVAN
Erie, Pa.
"Tangential Superfriction II:
Small Ball Don't Touch"
Sassafras, maple, cherry,
lacquer, acrylic
23 in. x 14 in. x 21 in.
Photo by Mark and
Debra Fainstein

JAY HOSTETLER
Athens, Ohio

Bowls
Quilted maple,
transparent lacquer
Yellow bowl: 1¾ x 13⅝-in. dia.
Cerise bowl: 1¾ x 10½-in. dia.
Photo by Chris Eaton

HELGA WINTER
Port Townsend, Wash.

Lathe-turned vessels
Madrone
4¼ in. x 6½-in. dia.
Photo by Roger Schrieber

ROBYN HORN
Little Rock, Ark.

"Pierced Geode"
Box-elder burl,
ebony, bloodwood
14 in. x 14 in. x 13 in.
Photo by Wesley Hitt

RICH SULLIVAN
Newport, Ore.

Ceremonial vessel form
Oregon maple burl,
alder, muslin
20 in. x 12-in. dia.
Photo by Dan Kvitka

MILAN FISKE
Burnt Hills, N.Y.

"Family"
Andiroba, maple
1½ in-dia. to 5½ in.-dia.
Photo by Milan Fiske

BARRY T. MACDONALD
Grosse Pointe, Mich.

Large bowl
Mahogany, tulipwood,
dyed veneers
6½ in. x 23-in. dia.
Photo by Barry T. Macdonald

PAM VOGT
Hampden, Mass.

"Nesting"
Western hemlock, ash
10 in. x 7-in. dia.
Photo by Xenophon A. Beake

MICHAEL D. MODE
New Haven, Vt.

"Rosewood Inhabitant"
Box-elder burl,
Indian rosewood
8 in. x 8 in. x 6 in.
Photo by Bob Barrett

BOB WILLIS
Pelahatchie, Miss.

Wooden vessel
Hackberry, cherry
30 in. x 12 in.
Photo by Steve Colston

ANDREW LAW BARNUM
Carmel, N.Y.

"Aviary Abode"
Pine, cherry
20 in. x 9½-in. dia.
Photo by Dennis and
Iona Elliott

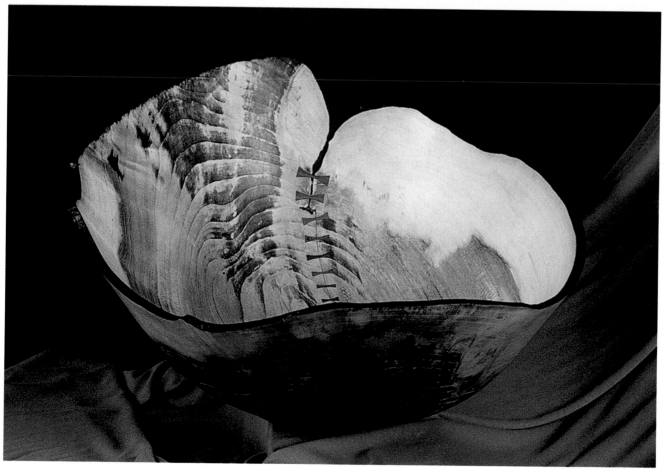

THOMAS KAMILA
Ashburnham, Mass.

Hollow oak vessel
Red oak
5⅛ in. x 6⅝-in. dia.
Photo by Ardy Kamila

JUDD MOSSER
East Aurora, N.Y.

"In Dreams We Have Spoken"
Sugar-maple gall
13 in. x 12 in. x 23½ in.
Photo by Dan Parucki

RON FLEMING
Tulsa, Okla.

"Datura"
Basswood
15 in. x 19-in. dia.
Photo by Hawks Photography

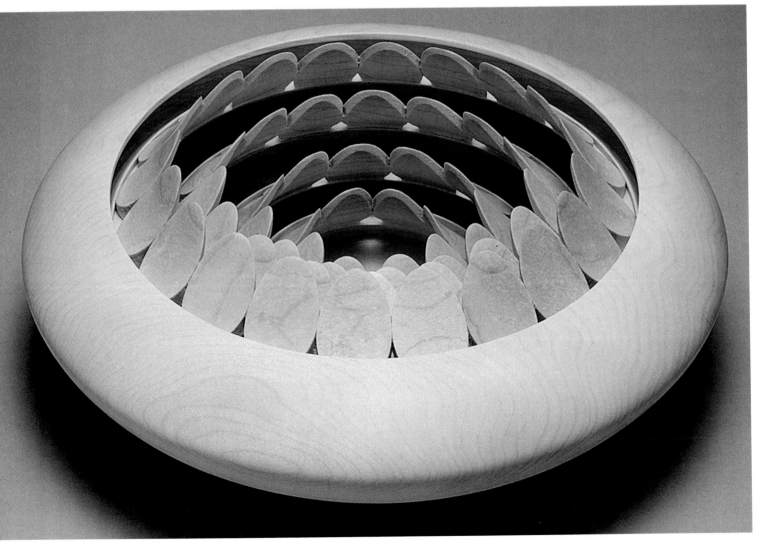

ROBERT M. STECKLER
Dallas, Tex.

Bowl
Cocobolo
5½ in. x 8½-in. dia.
Photo by Robin Sachs

RAY ALLEN
Yuma, Ariz.

Art object
Walnut, satinwood,
pernambuco, ziricote,
holly, birch
17½ in. x 19-in. dia.
Photo by Ray Allen

DENNIS ELLIOTT
Sherman, Conn.

"Wall Sculpture"
Bigleaf-maple burl, emerald-
jade avonite, metal, alabaster
33 in. x 2 in. x 27 in.
Photo by Dennis and
Iona Elliott

DEWEY GARRETT
Livermore, Calif.

"Opening #3"
Bleached maple
4 in. x 10-in. dia.
Photo by Jim Ferreira

JON N. SAUER
Daly City, Calif.

"Lines of Coco"
Cocobolo, ebony
2¾ in. x 5½ in. x 2¾-in. dia.
Photo by Richard Sargent

MICHAEL S. CHINN
Ames, Iowa

"TRI-16,000"
Mahogany, purpleheart,
aluminum, paint
10 in. x 6 in. x 7 in.
Photo by Peter Krumhardt

KERRY VESPER
Tempe, Ariz.

"Second Wave Bowl"
Birch plywood, African padauk
36 in. x 33 in. x 12 in.
Photo by Jeff Noble

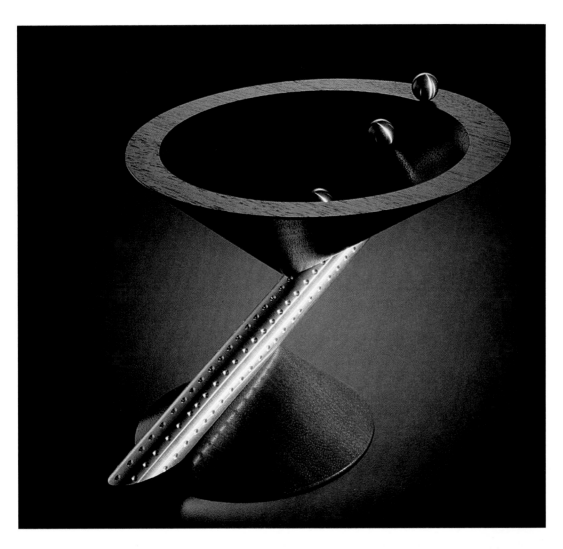

PETER PETROCHKO
Oxford, Conn.

"Amorphic Shape Vessel"
African zebrawood
20 in. x 20 in. x 16 in.
Photo by Frank Poole

WAYNE RAAB
Waynesville, N.C.

"3 Ball Plate"
Maple, cherry, acrylic lacquer
3½ in. x 14½-in. dia.
Photo by Wayne Raab

BONNIE KLEIN
Renton, Wash.

Chatterwork spin tops
Eastern maple colored
with felt pens
2 in. x 1¾-in. dia.
Photo by Mustafa Bilal

MIKE "CHAI" SCOTT
*Llanddeusant, Holyhead,
Anglesey, U.K.*

"Splash"
Oak
14 in. x 25-in. dia.
Photo by Hayley Smith

Accessories
&
Musical
Instruments

JEAN SOUMIS and
ALAIN LÉVESQUE
Saint-Mathias-sur-Richlieu,
Quebec, Canada

"Monte Bello"
Madrone burl, elm burl, curly
koa, ebonized maple,
stainless steel
19 in. x 7 in. x 11 in.
Photo by Clément Morin

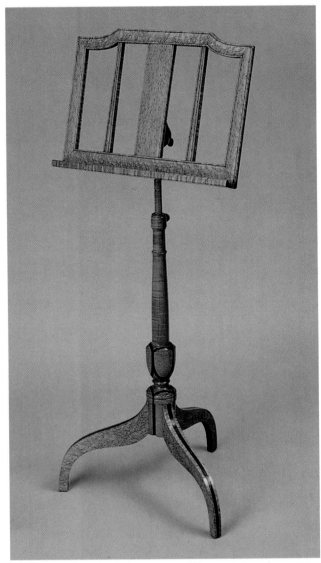

RICHARD GOURHAN
Seattle, Wash.

Violin
Spruce, maple, rosewood
8 in. x 2 in. x 24 in.
Photo by Rowland's Studio

LANCE PATTERSON
Boston, Mass.

Music stand
Maple, bird's-eye maple, walnut
20 in. x 43 in.
Photo by Lance Patterson

KENT EVERETT
Atlanta, Ga.

Four-string electric mandolin
Quilted maple, ebony
10 in. x 2 in. x 26 in.
Photo by Billy Howard

TOM BERRY
Chicago, Ill.

"Century"
Lyon and Healy commemorative
concert pedal harp
Maple, spruce,
ebony, satinwood
38 in. x 22 in. x 74 in.
Photo by Michael Tropea

MARK WESCOTT
Somers Point, N.J.

Steel-string guitar
Sitka spruce, Indian rosewood,
Honduras mahogany, ebony
15½ in. x 4½ in. x 43 in.
Photo by Mario Romo

KEVIN BURKE RILEY
Indianapolis, Ind.

Adjustable music stand
Ebonized walnut, bird's-eye
maple, brass, nylon, rubber
20 in. x 23 in. x 44 in.
Photo by David Calisch

VIC MATTHEWS
Coromandel, New Zealand

Lectern
Tawa, brass, rosewood
27½ in. x 17 in. x 48 in.
Photo by David Cook

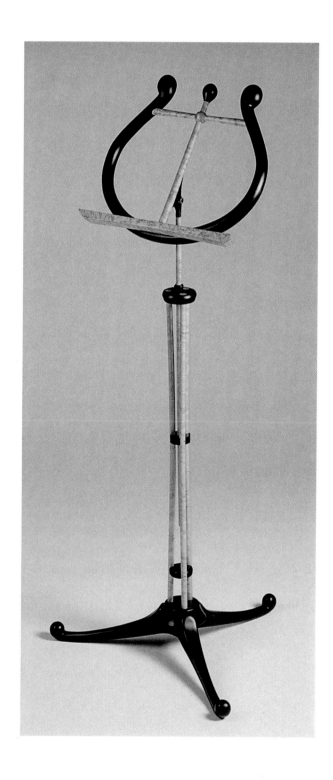

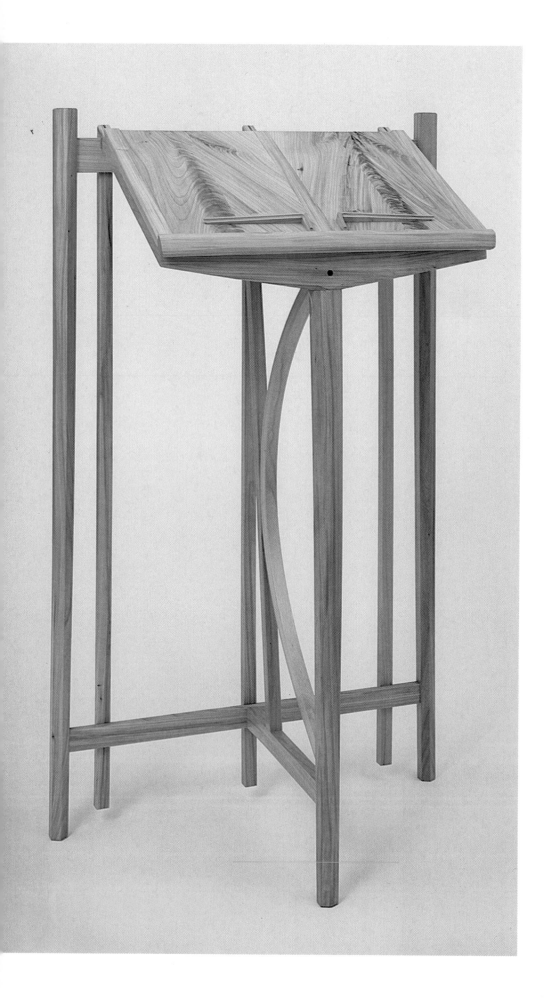

EVAN HUGHES
Brooklyn, N.Y.

Dictionary stand
American elm
32 in. x 24 in. x 56 in.
Photo by Edward Owen

KEVIN GILDERS
Melbourne, Victoria, Australia

Sousaphone
Huon pine, jarrah
48 in. x 24 in. x 24 in.
Photo by Fred Clappis

JONNY JAMES
Wellington, Telford,
Shropshire, England

"The Swan"
Music stand
English ash, American walnut
27 in. x 21 in. x 49 in.
Photo by Rory Williams

RION DUDLEY
Seattle, Wash.

Electric violin
Basswood, maple, ebony,
black lacquer, Plexiglas
20 in. x 9 in. x 3 in.
Photo by Rion Dudley

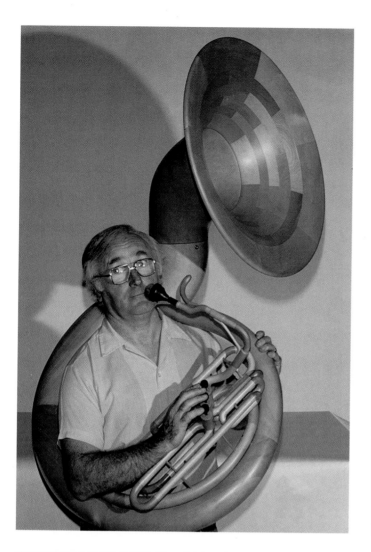

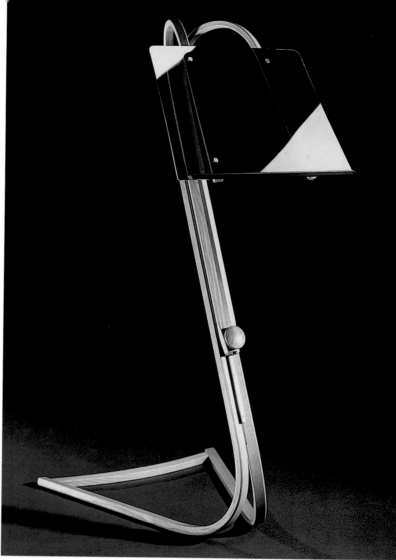

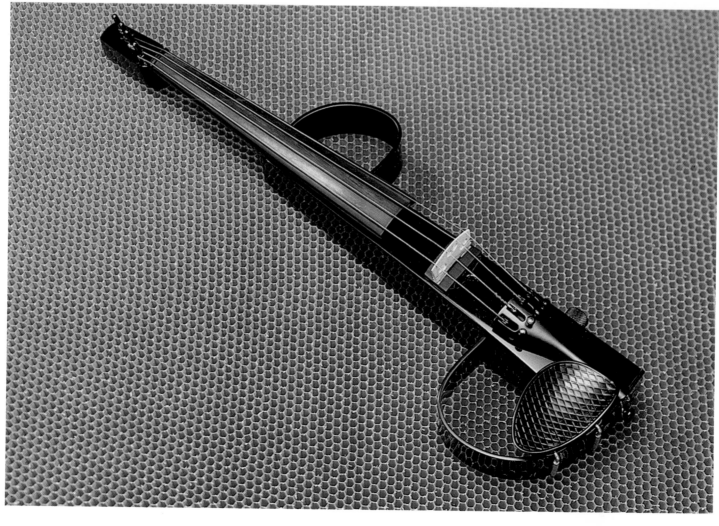

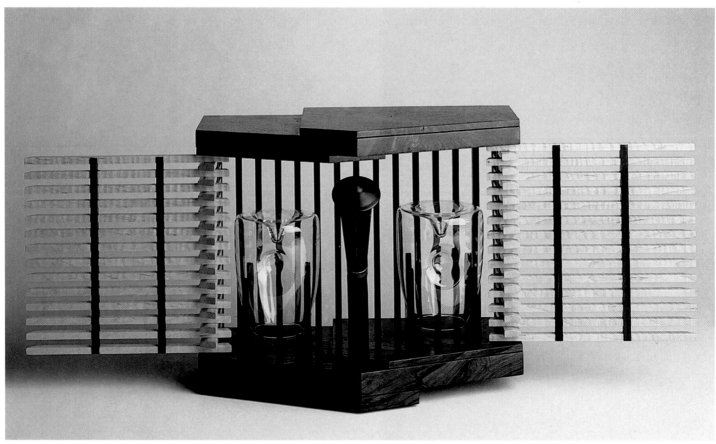

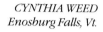

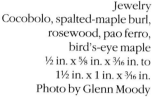

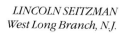

BARRY R. YAVENER
Buffalo, N.Y.

"Alyssa's Reality"
South American mahogany,
brass, 23k gold leaf
52 in. x 24 in. x 78 in.
Photo by Barry R. Yavener

CYNTHIA WEED
Enosburg Falls, Vt.

Jewelry
Cocobolo, spalted-maple burl,
rosewood, pao ferro,
bird's-eye maple
½ in. x ⅝ in. x 3/16 in. to
1½ in. x 1 in. x 3/16 in.
Photo by Glenn Moody

JOHN THOE
Seattle, Wash.

Basketweave mirror frame
Honduras mahogany
29 in. x 44 in.
Photo by John Curry

LEO KNAPP
N. Hollywood, Calif.

Wine-glass holder
Curly maple, English walnut,
macassar ebony
12 in. x 6 in. x 8 in.
Photo by Alan Shaffer

LINCOLN SEITZMAN
West Long Branch, N.J.

Petrified shopping basket
Ipe, cherry
15 in. x 9 in. x 18 in.
Photo by Jeff Martin

STEPHEN D. KNIGHT
Santa Rosa, Calif.

"Koa Lighthouse"
Hawaiian koa
30 in. x 15-in. dia.
Photo by Steve Carver

BARRY R. YAVENER
Buffalo, N.Y.

Floor lamps
American cherry, walnut, brass
74 in. x 20-in. dia.
Photo by Evan Sheppard

CHRIS BECKSVOORT
New Gloucester, Maine

"Candlever"
Cherry, pewter
20 in. x 5 in. x 7 in.
Photo by Kip Brundage

JIM SHAVER
Amelia, Va.

Spoon
Dogwood
2½ in. x 3 in. x 13 in.
Photo by Taylor Dabney

RION DUDLEY
Seattle, Wash.

Camera
Honduras mahogany, brass
12 in. x 6½ in. x 11 in.
Photo by Rion Dudley

JAMES E. GARNETT
Charlottesville, Va.

"Two Bees or Knot Two Bees"
Walnut, ebony, maple, koa,
butternut, persimmon
10¾ in. x 6¾ in. x 14½ in.
Photo by James E. Garnett

MICHAEL CULLEN
Petaluma, Calif.

"Fold Clock"
Buckeye, satinwood, ebony,
blue veneer, tiger-eye stone
6½ in. x 4½ in. x 12 in.
Photo by Mark Ross

FRANK EASTMAN
Dallas, Tex.

"Harmony Clock"
Mahogany, Hawaiian koa,
cherry, walnut, bird's-eye
maple, purpleheart, pink ivory
16½ in. x 7 in. x 24½ in.
Photo by Frank Eastman

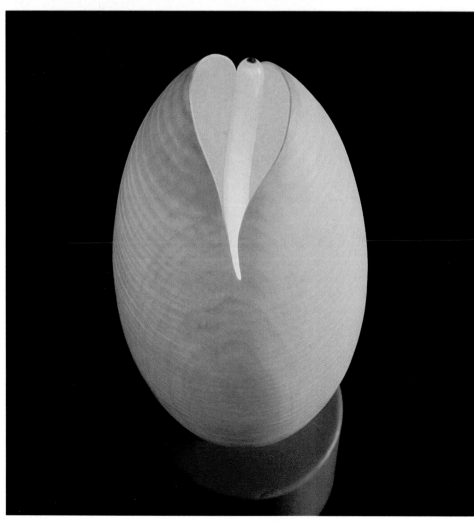

J. PAUL FENNELL
Topsfield, Mass.

"Fleur de Neon II"
Curly maple
11 in. x 4-in. dia.
Photo by Paul Lyden

ROBERT WINLAND
Cincinnati, Ohio

Lamp
Zebrawood, red oak,
boiré, lacewood, mahogany
24 in. x 24 in. x 78 in.
Photo by Robert Winland

DAVID HAZINSKI
Asheville, N.C.

Stepping stool
Walnut, oak
19 in. x 17 in. x 23 in.
Photo by David Hazinski

GLEN GURNER
Roslindale, Mass.

"Lighthouse IV"
Ash, maple, figured
anegre veneer, paint
11 in. x 11 in. x 17 in.
Photo by Charles Mayer

BRUCE SIEGEL
Milwaukee, Wis.

"Sugar Cube"
Teak, brass, Japanese paper
13 in. x 13 in. x 13 in..
Photo by Mike Schaefer

Woodworking Apprenticeship:
New Links in a Broken Chain

by Scott Landis

"As an apprentice it's all there...but you gotta read, look, listen and do. You have to be a verb."
—James Murdoch, graduate apprentice of the Rockport Apprenticeshop

In the lengthy apprenticeships of pre-industrial Europe, youths learned their trade by osmosis and endless repetition. Note the cooper's apprentice at far left in this 1704 Dutch illustration from Jan Luyken's Speigel van Het Menselyk bedryf. *(Courtesy The Winterthur Library: Printed Book and Periodical Collection.)*

On the day of his "freedom party," George Pettengell was 21 years old. He had just completed a six-year cooper's apprenticeship at Whitbread's Brewery in London, England, and was bracing himself for a traditional rite of passage. Plastered with horse manure, shavings and miscellaneous shop muck, Pettengell stood by as junior apprentices erected a hogshead around him. Stave by stave, the oak sides of the 38-in. high cask were hewn, shaved, heated and gathered into shape, and the iron rings were hammered down.

Once it was raised (and topped off with spent brewer's waste) the hogshead was knocked over and rolled two times the length of the shop floor with Pettengell trussed inside. At the end of his ride, he was dragged from the cask, tossed in the air and

Photos by Scott Landis, except where noted.

handed a fistful of beer. Master Lee — Pettengell's teacher, boss and role model those past six years — turned to his bedraggled apprentice and said, "Sonny, you can call me Ted."

This medieval ritual occurred in 1955, when George Pettengell took his place among the journeymen of the English cooper's trade. Through the endless repetition of a working apprenticeship, Pettengell had become proficient at the technical demands of his craft, and through osmosis he had absorbed its essential principles in ways that no academic exercise could match. Mastery would come later. "The key is the understanding of the material," Pettengell says. "The way the ax falls, the way you modify the stroke — that's artistry we can't understand." Even at Whitbread's, he notes, "only one in ten of us finished up as craftsmen. The others just made barrels."

Learning on the job, exchanging labor for instruction and practicing under a mentor — these are the pillars of apprenticeship. There are other, less demanding ways to learn how to work wood, perhaps more ways today than ever before. You can attend a craft-school program or a vocational institute. You can immerse yourself in back issues of *Fine Woodworking* magazine and study dozens of good books on the subject, or you can hone specific skills in one of a growing number of weekend workshops or short seminars that cover everything from boatbuilding to Windsor chairmaking. Although many of the traditional functions of apprenticeship have been dispersed among schools, government and trade unions, only the ancient model of apprenticeship marries the experience of learning and working with the intensity of a protracted, one-on-one exchange between a master craftsman and a novice.

Apprenticeship is cloaked by romantic half-truths and misconceptions. The institution has been lauded as the educational system that most closely resembles the parent/child relationship and vilified as a shameful relic of child labor. There's truth in both parallels, but the reality is a lot more complex. The successful apprenticeships I've examined represent a rich commingling of several distinct relationships: teacher/student, parent/child, master/servant, and employer/employee. Some of the most demanding, old-fashioned apprenticeships resemble slavery.

Much of America's woodworking heritage derives from England, but craftsmen trained in traditional apprenticeships as far apart as Europe and Japan have had experiences remarkably similar to George Pettengell's. Frank Klausz learned cabinetmaking in Hungary, in a formal, five-year apprenticeship with his father and at a state-run vocational school. "I paid the highest price for my trade," Klausz told me. "Once I apprenticed I didn't have a father, I had a master." (Klausz now trains his own apprentices, as described in the sidebar at right.) Makoto Imai learned his trade in a typical five-year Japanese apprenticeship to a house builder. It was a "slave-style" relationship, according to Imai, designed to break a youth's spirit and subordinate him to the master and the craft. Through the prism of hindsight, all old-world craftsmen I've met view their experience with the kind of admixture of pride and bitterness that soldiers reserve for boot camp. The very fact of their survival and their subsequent success in the trade validates the pain of their experience.

Such ordeals are almost unheard of today. After all, the apprenticeship system evolved to train pre-industrial tradesmen in the most efficient manner of manufacturing everyday objects of commerce and necessity. Factories now supply our needs, and the woodworking crafts survive mainly to service a luxury market or as a hobby. What's more, few modern craftsmen have the patience or discipline to submit to a five-year (or longer) program of voluntary servitude. Many of the links to our woodworking tradition have been crushed by industrialization. But when I recently examined some modern examples of informal (noninstitutional) craft education, I found vigorous and more flexible models of apprenticeship helping to reforge new links in that broken chain.

The Tradition

Learning a skill from one's parent must be the oldest form of apprenticeship, and prior to the 20th century, many youths learned to work wood from their fathers, uncles or older brothers. Whatever its informal precedents, the roots of apprenticeship were nourished by the medieval guilds and codified in English law in 1563, with the Statute of Artificers.

does what I want." Striking a balance between education and work is the cornerstone of a successful apprenticeship. "I've lost good people for being too hard on them," Klausz admits. "Maybe some of them left because I couldn't find the right balance."

There comes a time when every apprentice needs to find his own way. If he later returns, it often signals a development in skill and speed that could not have occurred in the master's shop. One of Klausz's former apprentices, Mike Knepp, went out on his own for almost a year, which Klausz now considers "the best thing that ever happened." When he came back as a regular employee, Knepp worked harder and faster and is now the top man in the shop. "Speed is an individual thing," says Klausz. "Mike learned to work quickly when he had to pay his own bills.

Klausz knows this lesson well, having put an ocean between himself and the father who trained him. Klausz was building a tall corner cupboard when his father paid a visit to his old garage workshop (Frank's first shop in this country). It was a challenging piece, and Klausz could have benefited from the old man's advice. But his father never offered any and Klausz never asked. By working out the problems on his own, Klausz says, "I grew up right in front of him."

Klausz's training was steeped in old-world "mystery." The elder Klausz held back many tricks of the trade—like a special dry joint used to make sharpening boxes—until Frank became a journeyman and, even then, swore him to secrecy. There are still things his father won't reveal. That's one aspect of the tradition Klausz is glad to leave behind. "I don't know which I enjoy more," he says, "making a beautiful piece of furniture or sharing the information."

Frank Klausz cut one stack of mahogany bank boxes, and his apprentice, Doug DeBue, is cutting the other (top photo). 'Once he's done with this open-dovetail assignment,' Klausz says, 'if he never cuts dovetails again for ten years, he's going to know how to do it.' Shown above is Klausz's current crew (left to right): Robert Pummill, former apprentice Michael Knepp, Edward Nightingale, apprentice Doug DeBue, John Darrow, James Travis and Frank Klausz.

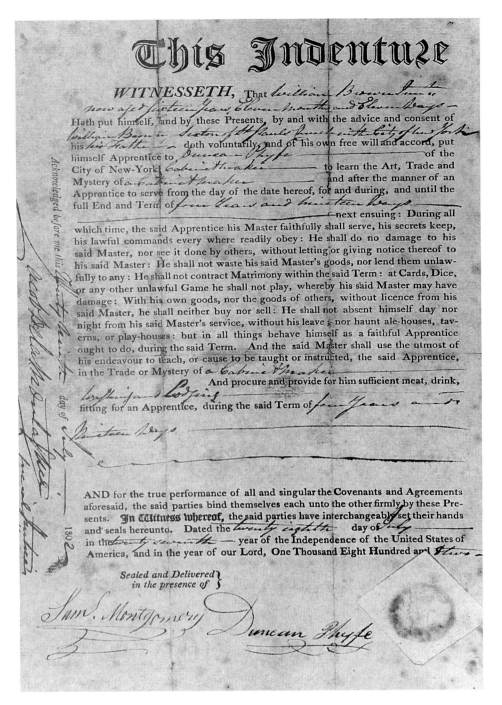

Standard contracts were commonly used to bind an apprentice to a master. With this certificate of indenture, dated July 28, 1802, William Brown was bound to New York cabinetmaker Duncan Phyfe for four years and 19 days, probably until the apprentice reached his 21st birthday. Brown would faithfully serve his master and keep his secrets, while Phyfe would provide food, clothing, lodging and teach him the 'Art, Trade and Mystery' of a cabinetmaker. (Courtesy Kendall H. Bassett.)

The statute established a seven-year learning period as a prerequisite to practicing a trade. This was considerably longer than the three-year to five-year term that prevailed on the continent, and it was meant to guarantee the quality of English manufactures. To join a guild as a journeyman and practice on his own for a daily wage an apprentice had to demonstrate his skill by completing a "master" piece. (The word "apprentice" derives from the French *apprendre, to* learn; the term "journeyman" comes from *journée,* which refers to a day's work, and does not imply that a journeyman had to travel.)

We think of apprenticeship as peculiar to the craft process, but virtually all occupations—from housewifery to farming—were conveyed by means of apprenticeship. Until 1752, the only way to acquire a medical education in America was by apprenticeship to a practicing physician. Traditional apprenticeship was inherently conservative, designed to perpetuate a social structure and limit access to the proprietary knowledge of the trades. Boilerplate indentures, like the one shown at left, commonly referred to the "Art, Trade and Mystery" of the master's craft and forbade the apprentice to engage in gambling, drinking, marriage or any other pleasurable activity that might tempt him from work.

As it was practiced in Britain and colonial America, the institution had four main purposes: to encourage education and literacy in general and the moral and religious education of youth in particular, to socialize orphans and poor children, to protect accomplished tradesmen from unfair competition by less-skilled workers, and to ensure a steady supply of well-trained labor.

Although the seven-year British contract (called an indenture because of its notched edge) was considered ideal in colonial America, it was not the norm. Four to seven years, terminating at the age of 21, was the most common length of colonial apprenticeship. Much shorter or longer terms were not unusual. At least one colonial carpenter's apprentice in Philadelphia was indentured for more than 30 years, and other terms have been recorded at less than one year. England's overabundance of labor and lack of resources promoted lengthy indentures, while in America the opposite conditions prevailed. These economic and geographic realities, in combination with a poorly developed legal system, created a social and political mobility in America that whittled away at the most conservative aspects of apprenticeship.

As Benno Forman pointed out in his book, *American Seating Furniture 1630-1740,* the scarcity of labor may have been good for colonial tradesmen, but it was hard on customers. In 1633, Governor John Winthrop of the Massachusetts Bay Colony objected to the excessive wages paid to tradesmen. In the same year, the General Court of the Massachusetts Bay Company ordered that "master carpenters, sawyers, masons...joiners...etc., should not receive more than two shillings a day without meals, and not more than fourteen pence a day...[with] board." Not long after, there were official complaints in Boston about shoddy workmanship as a result of truncated apprenticeships. A petition was filed in 1677 by Boston artisans who found themselves "under great disadvantages by the frequent Intruding of Strangers from all parts."

Notwithstanding such grievances, American statutes were doomed to fail for many of the same reasons as the English laws. Records of the *Privy Council Register* in London (1669) note that the Statute of Artificers "has been by most of the Judges looked upon as inconvenient to trade and to the increase of inventions." The decline of apprenticeship was further hastened in America by waves of immigration and war, when access to European imports was restricted by British blockades and there was a ready demand for the military services of unskilled young men.

Until the 19th century, apprenticeship was a primary source of basic education. Masters were often expected to instruct their apprentices in reading, writing and arithmetic, but their inability to fulfill these obligations contributed to the demand for itinerant schoolmasters and night schools and eventually led to public education. With the advent of compulsory education and industrialization, the character of the master/apprentice relationship changed dramatically. Masters no longer had to educate, clothe or house their wards, and machinery began to perform the most repetitive tasks of the young apprentice, such as ripping or planing stock and cutting joints. Apprentices became cheap labor and were more likely to sweep floors or operate machinery than work wood.

Along with the rise in literacy and public education came an increase in printed trade books, which tended to dispel some of whatever "mystery" remained to the practice of the trades. (The word "mystery" derives from the classical Greek *mystoss*, which refers to silence and ceremony. In archaic usage, it was probably conflated with the middle French *maistre*, or master, and *métier*, or trade.) Most of these early handbooks were meant to augment, rather than replace, conventional craft education, and they rarely instruct in the step-by-step manner of a modern how-to text. But Batty Langley's pocket-sized guide to building construction, *The Builder's Jewel: Or, the Youth's Instructor, and Workman's Remembrancer* (London,

1746), suggests that by the 18th century the apprenticeship system was in serious peril. In his introduction, Langley explains that the book is intended chiefly for "apprentices, who may be absolutely unacquainted with this noble art, and are so unfortunate...to be bound to jobbing masters, who know but little...." By studying his book, Langley suggests they may "make themselves such masters herein, that few masters are able or willing to make them." Lest his work be considered subversive by the practicing masters of the trade, Langley adds a final plea that it "be no affront to the sage workman, by re-informing him of those rules which have slipt his memory, and informing him of others which he never knew...."

Written records of cabinetmaking apprenticeships are hard to come by. One of the few surviving documents is a 140-page journal, kept by Edward Jenner Carpenter, an apprentice at the Miles & Lyons cabinetshop in Greenfield, Massachusetts, between 1842 and 1847. Carpenter records observations and events that took place during the third and fourth years of his apprenticeship. Although he was already building substantial pieces of furniture on his own, the lack of any direct reference to his first two years makes it hard to draw conclusions about his early training. Still, the journal yields a vivid portrait of one rather benevolent 19th-century apprenticeship.

Carpenter's daily routine was rigorous but flexible. From September to April, he worked until 9 p.m. six days a week (work quit three hours earlier in summer). But he took long weekends to visit relatives or even to collect maple sap or go fishing. Many evenings and Sundays were spent reading in the shop or attending social gatherings about town. He boarded with one of the shop masters but had considerable freedom of association, often inviting other apprentices to share his bed when the junior apprentice (his normal sleeping partner) was ill or out of town.

References to shop work are sporadic and perfunctory, as in this entry for March 14, 1844: "I finished the Bureau today that I begun a week ago last Monday and began another just like it & I hope it will not take quite as long to make it." As time goes on, the seemingly endless routine of bureaus and secretaries (about one every two weeks) takes its toll. Carpenter grouses: "I began another cheap Butternut Secratary this morning it is Bureaus & Secratary all the

time I have worked on them about a year & I begin to think it is about time to learn to make something else." Not long after, he writes again: "I finished a Secratary today & begun another just like it, & I hope it is the last." Regarding the hierarchy of shop work, he notes, "begun the Secratary but did not do much to it Dexter [the junior apprentice] was carrying in boards & [I] had to kick the lath[e] in his place." On August 4, 1844, he looks forward longingly to his release: "To day is my 19th birth day, 2 years & I am my own man."

Edward Carpenter's experience teetered between traditional apprenticeship and wage labor. By the middle of his term, he was paid for piece work and was engaged in "stints," or short-term contracts, which required him to complete a job within a predetermined number of days. "These times are hard times for Cabinet Journeymen," Carpenter recorded in 1844, and within a decade or two apprenticeship was all but extinct as a mainstream mechanism for educating young craftsmen. For the next hundred years, the institution would cling to survival on the few sheltered islands of artisanry that remained above the rising tide of industry.

The Cooper's Apprentice

George Pettengell learned the "business of coopering" on one such sheltered island. He grew up in London after the Second World War and, at the age of 15, became an apprentice at Whitbread's Brewery. Pettengell had no burning desire to be a cooper—it was a family tradition. His father and grandfather had been coopers, and young George was never consulted. (He later helped train his brother, Jim, who is shown in the top photo on p. 166.)

Pettengell spent his first six months in the mill shop, where hazing was routine. Apprentices were dumped in the shavings, locked in the bathrooms and trapped in the steam boxes. The most rebellious among them would get his penis painted for good measure. Having proved his mettle, Pettengell was placed under the tutelage of Master Lee, and his apprenticeship began in earnest.

George (nicknamed "Muscles") and his three fellow apprentices ("Inky," "Tadpole" and "Winkle") began work at 7:05 a.m.—about ten minutes before Master Lee showed up. Work ended at

Tradesmen at Colonial Williamsburg are trained in a six-year apprenticeship program that replicates (albeit more gently) some aspects of the traditional experience. Jim Pettengell is a journeyman cooper at Williamsburg and was the last to serve a formal apprenticeship under Master Ted Lee at Whitbread's Brewery in London.

breweries, factories and shippers. Coopers were among the highest-paid workers in the country. But when Pettengell left England for the United States in 1967, the breweries had turned to stainless steel and the days of traditional cooperage were rapidly coming to a close.

The Williamsburg Apprentice

Now, George Pettengell is Master Cooper at Colonial Williamsburg in Virginia, where apprentices are trained in the traditional hand methods he learned in his youth. As you might expect, it's a modified program (I imagine Williamsburg frowns on hazing) more suited to older apprentices who have an academic background and are responsible for interpreting the past at a living-history museum. Pettengell admits that "there's no comparison with the concentration of work" he experienced at Whitbread's, but he continues, "I like to think the apprentices here are challenged. It's a discipline...sometimes the only way to learn is to have someone tell you 'This is the way it's done.'"

In the Anthony Hay shop at Colonial Williamsburg there is one cabinetmaking apprentice and two journeymen, in addition to an apprentice and a journeyman harpsichord maker. All of them are responsible to Mack Headley, modern master of the shop. Williamsburg apprentices undergo a six-year training program, with specific expectations attached to each skill. Headley has divided these into six separate categories: fundamentals, structural design/practice, decorative design/practice, structural design/theory, decorative design/theory, and finishing. Each skill is further subdivided (for example, fundamental skills include wood technology, tool technology and wood preparation) and is assigned a numerical factor of difficulty and an

When he turned 21 years old, George Pettengell (in the barrel) was initiated with considerable fanfare into the London Fraternity of Coopers. Pettengell's master, Ted Lee, looks on from the rear. (Courtesy George Pettengell.)

5:00 p.m., with standard breaks for breakfast, lunch and tea. The first-year apprentice began with simple cutting and shaping of parts, getting used to the broad ax, drawknife and jointer plane — a large, upside-down wooden plane — and developing the strength and coordination he would need later on. During that time, Pettengell received a few dollars a week for pocket money and, at the end of the year, was enrolled in technical courses at London College for one day a week.

When he turned 18, Pettengell "went on halves." Still working under Master Lee, he was paid for half the value of each barrel, hogshead or firkin he made. At 20, Pettengell "went on two-thirds" until his 21st birthday, when he was ushered into the Fraternity of Coopers with the initiation described earlier. From that point on, he was permitted to use machinery — a bandsaw for cutting ends, a jointer for smoothing staves and an electric drill. But to qualify as a journeyman, he had to pass a day-long practical exam. A master's certificate required three more years of practice and another ceremony.

At the beginning of Pettengell's term, in 1950, there were as many as 500 coopers and two dozen apprentices in the greater London area making all manner of wooden casks for the city's anticipated level of mastery at the end of each year. Interest in the program is so intense that the number of applications for a recent cabinetshop position was cut off at 65.

Apprentices with prior woodworking experience are evaluated after 90 days to determine their skill level, but most start by sizing lumber—hand planing it flat and square—before cutting dovetails. They move on to mortise-and-tenon joinery, and add proportion, sculpting, tool maintenance and so on wherever they can along the way. True to the 18th-century tradition, there's a lot of repetitious hand work, which affords an intimate understanding of wood surfaces, grain and texture. To gain some of the "real-world" experience of running a business, Williamsburg artisans are encouraged to practice their craft at home.

The regular interpretive demands of the museum interrupt the apprentice's focus and retards his the training, but the structure helps maintain a coherent program. When I visited the Hay shop recently, apprentice Chris Wright was squaring lumber for a set of 12 chairs, which Headley expected to keep him busy for months. On the first two or three chairs, Wright spent 45 minutes flattening and squaring each piece of stock, but he's picking up speed. In time, he'll lay out the mortises, which will be chopped by journeymen Kaare Lofthiem and David Salisbury. Later on, Wright will rough shape the front legs, and the journeymen will finish them off. Headley allows that chairmaking is probably not the best place to start an apprentice—it's a real challenge to the cabinetmaker's art and is a specialty of its own—but Wright had years of experience as a gunsmith and is learning quickly under the tutelage of the journeymen.

In the absence of machinery, Headley explains, "eye judgment is a real important part of 18th-century training." His own study of period furniture suggests that although pieces made in the same shop usually exhibit superficial similarities in design, closer examination often reveals very different construction techniques. This would suggest that the master was responsible for the artwork but permitted subtle variations in construction, perhaps brought to the shop by journeymen trained elsewhere. Through this kind of analysis, Headley says, "I think we're getting closer to what 18th-century cabinetmaking was...a really sophisticated, technical profession."

When East Meets West

If Mack Headley cultivates the eye, timber framer Makoto Imai puts his trust in the body. "The mind forgets easily," Imai says, "but the body remembers." He compares an apprentice to tempered steel: "Heat it up, pound it, cool it off; heat it up, pound it, cool it off." Having forged his own body in a traditional Japanese apprenticeship, Imai's criteria for apprentices are more intuitive than objective. The ideal apprentice, he explains, is quiet but not too intellectual ("talking bothers body"), alert and attentive (stands straight "like a dog") and well focused (has a "sharp face").

Absent from Imai's list is any prerequisite experience or manual dexterity. In fact, he believes that craftsmen are built from within. A Japanese carpenter has a lot to learn—about wood, tools and architecture—but given the basic ingredients, the skill will take care of itself. "Technical is not the most important," Imai once told me. "Some people use only their head to learn, but the body has to learn, too. After 25 years I'm still learning."

Imai grew up in the rural district of Hida, Japan, and knew from an early age that he would be a carpenter. According to Zen custom, if a young man wants to become a monk, he must sit at the gates of the monastery until he is noticed. Imai took every opportunity to watch carpenters at work and even borrowed their tools to practice. His perseverance paid off when, at the age of 15, his mother arranged for him to become a carpenter's apprentice. He rode his bicycle to work, carrying lumber on his shoulder, and he put in long hours raking and burning sawdust, sorting nails and learning to sharpen before he was allowed to chop his first mortise. Even then, he could not shave the joint to a line.

Three years into his apprenticeship, Imai's master gave him a decent set of chisels, some marking and measuring tools and a sharpening stone and plane. At that point, he began to get seriously involved with the work, doing all his own mortises and learning different joints. He continued to progress until the end of his fifth year, when he was given a simple house to lay out by himself. At his mother's behest, Imai "donated" a sixth year of work to his master.

Since he moved to Northern California in the 1970s, Imai has had about six apprentices for varying lengths of time. The one who stayed the longest was Bruce Dichter, an ex-carpenter from Minnesota, who saw in Imai "the truest craftsman, the one most submitted to his work." Dichter hung around the shop for four months, watching and trying to help out, until Imai turned to him one day and said, "Oh yeah, you're an apprentice now." Dichter was 35 at the time, and a traditional apprenticeship was already precluded by two kids, a wife and about 20 years. But Dichter sold off his back issues of *Fine Woodworking* and *Fine Homebuilding* (Imai says, "Too much study from books is not useful") and moved to the Shasta-Trinity National Forest, where Imai and his family were living in an aluminum house trailer and setting up shop. "I don't think either of us knew what we were in for," Dichter says.

Dichter is not a natural craftsman. "My hands are clumsy," he admits. Helping to carry *shoji* screens to an installation, he accidentally ripped the rice paper. Dichter was mortified, but if Imai was annoyed he didn't let on. "It was difficult to really trust that I would learn," Dichter says. The low wages and submissive behavior were hard—on his savings and family, as well as his ego—but he hoped, in time, that his mind would relax and his body would take over. "Americans want to know exactly what you're going to teach, one to ten," Imai says. Dichter tried to restrain himself. He did what he was told and watched Imai out of the corner of his eye. If he had a question, Dichter would approach the master, clear his throat and wait to be acknowledged.

Hand tools are Imai's primary training vehicle. Noting the inroads made by machinery here and in Japan, he cautions his apprentices to seek a balance. "You have to use some machinery," Imai tells them. "Thirty percent is great; 50 percent is a little bit easier, but there's less enjoyment." So he accepts one job at a time and does most of the resawing and thickness planing himself, affording his apprentices and employees the maximum exposure to hand tools and materials. If this doesn't prepare them to earn a living, Imai makes no apologies. "That's not my responsibility," he says simply.

The duration of an apprenticeship depends upon the apprentice and the projects he is able to work on, but Imai

Makoto Imai takes tea with his apprentice Bruce Dichter (left) and employee Gary Bella (right) in his shop in Northern California. The Bay-Area house shown below took Imai and company almost two years to build. Every timber was wrapped individually with paper to protect it from fingerprints and damage in transit from shop to site. The paper and cornstarch glue were stripped away from the joints during construction so they wouldn't interfere with the fit. (Photo by Makoto Imai.)

figures it takes twice as long to train an American in an American environment. If most woodworkers are too independent for Imai's taste, Dichter was too compliant. "I want a little bit of both," Imai says. Dichter thought the apprenticeship could go on forever, but by the end of five years, it was evident — "especially to Makoto-san," Dichter says — that he had to find his own niche.

When I visited Dichter recently, he had moved several hours south of Imai and fixed up a small plywood shop behind his house. It was newly outfitted with the machinery Imai recommended. He hoped to integrate the Japanese tools and techniques with Western-style carpentry, and if he works with Imai again, Dichter explained, it won't be as an apprentice. "That phase is finished."

Apprenticeship, for Imai, never ends. Some of his former apprentices now teach, and he's arranged work in Japan

for several others. One recent apprentice was so lonely and distracted that Imai packed him off to Japan to work and find a wife. "Sixteen years ago, I started teaching in the Bay Area and the energy was great," Imai says, "but now, the energy is a little bit less. People don't understand how much it takes.... This kind of work is whole-life learning."

Dennis Young is the only Westerner I know to have enrolled in a traditional Japanese woodworking apprenticeship. Young spent four years in the early 1970s learning to make furniture in Central Japan, and he said of his experience: "I never really enjoyed it...the lack of privacy, the rigors...but the level of skill was so high. I just had this burning desire to be a craftsman." After that, he apprenticed for another two years to an English chairmaker.

In Japan, Young worked ten-hour days, six days a week, plus half a day on Sunday. Like Imai, he spent months orienting his body to the tools and absorbing fundamental skills like sharpening. In a 1987 *Fine Woodworking* magazine article, Young is quoted as saying: "Everyone [in the shop] referred to learning as 'stealing' techniques. Your teacher would show you the basics...but you were expected to learn the fine points by observing." It was a year and a half before his work was good enough to join the regular production.

Young has his share of gory tales—of his master's neglect and abuse, and of cleaning toilets after all-night sake binges. Dramatic as they may be, he now finds such stories indulgent and tedious. "Fundamental aspects of my training live with me every day in the shop," he wrote recently in a letter from Japan. "The longer I do this work the more commonsensical the education seems to be. The fact that it was severe or took place a distance from home doesn't seem an important aspect of the equation."

Young married a Japanese woman and moved back to Japan in 1991, but during the 12 years or so that he designed and built furniture in Northern California, he took on several apprentices of his own. He found the experience distracting and did not seek them out—they came to him. Charles Tilt was attracted to Young's hand-tool aesthetic and his "incredible ability" and he became Young's apprentice in 1983. It was a loose arrangement at the start, with no pay, no clear term and few expectations. "Neither of us were very communicative," Tilt explains. Young taught him the way he had learned, by example rather than explanation. He wanted Tilt to keep a journal and serve tea to guests, and he explained procedures only once. Still, compared to Young's experience, Tilt was on the fast track. Where Young spent six months learning to sharpen, Tilt did it in three.

Young's nonverbal approach and his emphasis on perfection often frustrated Tilt, who had a "tremendous desire to see the end product." Eight months into his apprenticeship, Tilt convinced Young to let him build a Windsor rocker. (He was working nights and weekends in a restaurant to make ends meet and insisted that he needed to sell the chair to survive.) After about a year, Tilt was exhausted and was losing track of his

long-term goals; Young was having personal difficulties of his own. When the tension erupted in bitter accusations, Tilt left the shop. "I somehow muddled through," he recalls, "although I had never made a piece from beginning to end without Dennis's supervision." It took Tilt two years to go back, but he brought Young an offering: a small stool, meticulously executed with traditional Japanese joinery.

Tilt's work continues to evolve, but there are similarities in their style that the years and bitterness can't erase. The hallmarks are clean, crisp design, uncompromising execution and subtle, expressive details. "I started with what I was given," Tilt says, "and I'd have a hard time making a radical change." Despite the rigors and frustrations, Tilt admits that the system worked. "Dennis felt—and I think rightly so—that you learn best by discovery and by doing." Although he had nightmares about Young for years, Tilt cherishes the mentor relationship: "He had a huge impact on my life, in positive and negative ways...it's something I miss even now." In the end, Tilt says, "I learned to appreciate the process, as opposed to the final result."

Dennis Young (at right) spent four years as an apprentice in a Japanese furniture company before moving to England to learn Windsor chairmaking. Charles Tilt (below) apprenticed to Young for an intense and tumultuous 14 months.

Sculpting an Apprenticeship

Legend has it that when Northwest carver Mungo Martin was an infant, his elders bound his eyelashes in a paintbrush in an attempt to foster his artistic tendencies. He was also put inside of a box drum to encourage him to sing. Martin went on to become a Kwakiutl artist and chief of considerable renown, who did most of his carving during the first half of this century, when native culture was either dormant or in decline. He was one of a handful of natives who helped sustain both the ceremony and artistic tradition that are so tightly interwoven in the Pacific Northwest.

Martin died in 1962, but not before he had passed the knowledge gained from his stepfather to his son-in-law and grandsons, and thereby to an entire generation of artists and carvers. According to Bill Holm, curator emeritus of the Burke Museum in Seattle, the "magical ways of inducing talent" used by Martin's elders were but one way native children were introduced to the crafts; apprenticeship was another. In a recent conversation I had with Holm, he explained that apprenticeship to an uncle or grandparent was "pretty much standard procedure, at least in the northern two-thirds of the coast," where rank and privilege followed matrilineal descent.

Robert Davidson is an heir to that tradition, having been strongly influenced by his grandparents and by the classic work of his great-grandfather, Charles Edensaw. Davidson started carving with his father when he was 13 years old and then went to work with his grandfather. When he was 20, he worked with the eminent Haida sculptor Bill Reid for about a year. Steeping himself in the culture, Davidson visited museums and went door to door in search of traditional art. When he could borrow an example he liked, he slept with it next to his bed.

"I went through many styles before I developed my own," Davidson says, and in a 1979 retrospective exhibition of prints at the University of British Columbia, he divided his work into four stages of growth: apprentice, journeyman, master and artist. During his apprentice phase, which Davidson calls "learning the alphabet," he copied old images to explore traditional balance and proportion. Many craftsmen are reluctant to copy, but Davidson asserts: "There's nothing wrong with copying, as long as you don't claim it.... You've got to sing other people's songs before you can write your own." As a journeyman ("interpreting the song"), he pursued variations on these traditional forms, and as a master ("mapping new worlds") he experimented boldly with new

principles of design. As an artist, he draws upon his own internal imagery.

Davidson took his first apprentices in 1976 to help carve a house front in honor of Charles Edensaw. A year later, he had eight apprentices, working on four 13-ft. totem poles. It was an experience from which he took six months to recover. "I was pretty rough in the beginning," Davidson says, "but it's the only way I knew." All told, he's had 17 apprentices in about as many years, but only four of them have been long term.

Just as Davidson considers each piece to be practice for the one that follows, every apprentice paved the way for the next. He became more patient and the apprenticeship—like his art—became more structured. On one large project, he had three apprentices and needed them all to move a pole. When two kept showing up late, he phoned a local university professor to ask how she handled tardiness. "We ignore it," she said.

From then on, Davidson made punctuality a requirement. To cut down on "dead weight," he has since added a written application, a resumé, an interview and letters of recommendation to the admission process. In four pages of printed matter, he lists the qualifications, job description and curriculum for an apprentice carver. (He prefers to train Haida, but he'll accept other natives and whites.) Among other things, a candidate must take direction and be willing to work 35 hours a week for at least two years. The curriculum outlines a formidable list of personal and technical skills, from budgeting and verbal communication to carving a totem pole in the traditional Haida style. "For your art to progress," Davidson says, "you have to progress as a person."

The structure of Davidson's current program provides a flexibility that a more casual apprenticeship might not support. When I visited his current apprentice, Gloria Goodrich, she was living in Everett, Washington—about two hours south of Davidson's studio—and commuting three days a week. The

Sculptor Robert Davidson uses apprenticeship to help revive Haida tradition and art in the Pacific Northwest.

Working on her living-room floor, apprentice Gloria Goodrich attaches cedar-bark rope and goat fur to a Robert Davidson transformation mask. The body of the mask is a paper casting with a red cedar backboard and operculum shells for teeth.

This 1990 mask, 'Dawning of the Eagle,' is Davidson's self-portrait. It's made of red cedar, acrylic, operculum shell, flicker feathers and human hair, and measures 9 in. x 12 in. x 7½ in. (Courtesy Inuit Gallery of Vancouver, Canada; photo by Trevor Mills.)

rest of the time she works at home on assignments like the transformation mask shown above. Goodrich says the admission process took almost a year to complete and, with daily pilgrimages to the mailbox, it was fraught with all the anxiety of a college application.

For the first few months, Goodrich worked mainly on painting. Her first carving was the back of a mask that Davidson was completing with his senior apprentice, Larry Rosso. Davidson likes to have two apprentices at different levels of development, so that the more advanced one can help train the novice. Goodrich went on to sharpen and implant teeth, attach hair and make rope out of cedar bark. Step by step, she's being introduced to the finer points of carving wood. Davidson has also worked on design and has introduced Rosso and Goodrich to the business side of the craft — how to bid a job.

Carving takes place in three stages. It begins with roughing, when the major planes are defined. Next, the eye sockets, cheeks and other body parts are shaped. Finally, the form is finished and detailed, and any paint, hair, shells or feathers are added. Goodrich hasn't gotten this far, but at each stage, Davidson will complete one-half of the work and expect Goodrich to match it. (Davidson's study of old totem poles suggests that this was a traditional practice; most poles are bilaterally symmetrical, but on many one side appears to have been carved by a less experienced hand than the other.) He will check her work and clean it up or deepen it before allowing her to progress to the next stage.

Davidson started Goodrich at $5 per hour, but she asked him to figure out at the end of each week how much her work was worth. She was there to learn and didn't like to feel rushed. Now, Davidson pays her by the piece or $50 per color on a standard mask paint job. To develop speed and confidence, she hopes to extend the apprenticeship to three years, perhaps even four or five. "It's been a year already," Goodrich says, "and it seems like I've barely touched it."

"We kill ourselves by hoarding knowledge," Davidson says, "but sometimes I give too much. Apprenticeship is like having two jobs." Husbanding his resources, he decided not to take on another apprentice after Rosso completed his three-year term. But when he hired Rosso back recently to help carve a pole, Davidson realized the benefit of working with a competent journeyman he'd trained. "We can talk in a jargon I don't have to explain," Davidson says. "I can say 'This is what I want' and he can work it out."

If apprenticeship has been a means to repair the broken links of the craft tradition in America, for Davidson it is helping to reconstitute the Haida culture itself. Through his graphics, and especially his carvings (which are often inaugurated by ritual dance and song), Davidson gives life to ancient myths and traditions. "It's taken me a long time to acquire the knowledge," Davidson says, "and it'll take me a lot longer to give it away."

Art Espenet Carpenter is a founder and guiding spirit of the Baulines Crafts Guild, based in Sausalito, California. He's had more than 100 apprentices in the last 20 years, several of whom have had apprentices of their own.

Apprenticeship California Style

Six months out of college, with a degree in finance and the economy skidding into recession, Mason Rapaport took a hard look at his options. Prospects in real estate and banking were grim, so he decided to revive an old interest in woodworking, which he had enjoyed for years as a hobby in his father's shop. With nowhere else to turn, he sent letters to about 20 different woodworking programs across the country. But Rapaport wasn't anxious to go back to school. He says, "I was looking for someone who would let me into his shop, let me work on his furniture and let me build a project on my own."

Rapaport found all three in the apprenticeship program of the Baulines Crafts Guild (BCG), a nonprofit, multimedia craft organization based in Sausalito, California. It was the least formal institution he approached, but Rapaport liked its flexible "contract learning program," in which the personality, skills and goals of an apprentice are matched with those of a practicing craft master. Founded in 1972 in the coastal village of Bolinas — a former whaling station turned artist's colony — the program was designed to offer people with some craft experience the "feel" of a working shop.

Art Espenet Carpenter was one of the guild's five founders, and he still lives and works across from the lagoon on the road to Bolinas. "It really was an outgrowth of the sixties," Carpenter says, "where everybody wanted to leave IBM and go to the woods." Rather than abandon novices to their idealism, the apprenticeship program offered a kind of career map and compass. In the woodworking schools, Carpenter explains, students might take six months to build a chair. "Here, they have to do it in three days."

Carpenter's public profile has given a presence to the guild, and his no-nonsense attitude has helped to shape the apprenticeship program. There is a one-page application and a one-page contract; after an initial screening, apprentices deal directly with the masters. Although Carpenter was the only founding woodworker, today roughly half of the guild masters are furniture makers, including several of his former apprentices. Over the years, more than 100 apprentices have passed through Carpenter's shop, although he estimates that fewer than 10 percent of them stay in the trade. "Quite a few come with no intention of being a woodworker," he says. For those who do, Carpenter considers the BCG program a "jet assist."

According to Lynn Learned, executive director of the BCG, most candidates have a "developed interest" in the craft. Learned interviews them all to ensure that they have the basic skills and motivation to take advantage of the program. Apprentices are required to have prior training in shop safety and, if she suspects an applicant lacks sufficient experience or shop savvy, she might recommend a short workshop or a course at a community college. If they're looking for a more structured environment or accreditation, Learned refers them to North Bennet Street School, College of the Redwoods or another similar institution.

Participation doesn't come cheap. A BCG apprenticeship costs $750 per month, plus an annual $25 associate membership fee. But unlike college tuition, up to one-third of the basic fee can be earned back by working at minimum wage on a master's projects. (Associate membership entitles apprentices to participate in guild exhibitions, studio tours, weekend seminars and other programs.) Masters receive a "teaching stipend" of between $100 and $600 per month, depending on how much time the apprentice devotes to the master's work. Apprentices are covered by workers'-compensation insurance, and the BCG carries a full liability insurance package for its directors and masters. According to Learned, the program remains unaccredited to maintain its flexibility. "There's a real need for a noninstitutional education," she says. "The kind of thinking that comes from working in three dimensions and problem solving is ignored in the school system."

Roger Heitzman (at right) confers with his employee, Michael Gerlach (left), whose production experience complements Heitzman's skill as a designer/craftsman.

Three months is the basic time unit, although many apprentices stay for six months or longer. "Everything has to do with the articulated goals of the student," Learned explains. By prior arrangement, they can mix and match masters, spending a month or two with one and several months with another. Apart from the technical skills of woodworking, which can be learned well enough from a book or at a weekend seminar, an effective master must also provide an introduction to design and business. "In three months," Carpenter tells prospective apprentices, "you're going to pick up the style of your teacher. Then you go home and practice for the next 20 years. Don't practice on my time."

The success of any apprenticeship rests heavily on the master, and a current list of about 25 BCG masters includes Bay-Area heavyweights such as John and Carolyn Grew-Sheridan and Garry Knox Bennett. The actual number of available teaching masters varies from time to time, but all are practicing professionals who have made a living from their craft for at least five years and whose work has been recognized by a gallery or museum exhibition. To be admitted to the guild, they must be sponsored by a current BCG craft master and have their work evaluated by a jury.

Rapaport studied the masters' statements in the BCG literature and was intrigued by Roger Heitzman's description of furniture that would "enhance yet transcend function." He also liked the fact that Heitzman was a full-time woodworker and not a teacher. He checked Heitzman's work in *Fine Woodworking* magazine and, somewhat sheepishly, asked to see a portfolio. (Apart from any investment of time and money, Rapaport would have to relocate from Lake George, New York, to California, so he was understandably cautious.) Heitzman had been anxious to get an apprentice, and he was happy to oblige. When the photos arrived, Rapaport said, "This is great—this is where I want to go."

The apprenticeship got underway in July of 1990 at Heitzman's well-equipped shop in Scott's Valley. Heitzman has an industrial-arts degree from Humboldt State College, but scooped together most of what he knows about woodworking in the 15 years since he graduated. Drawing on magazine articles and Ernest Joyce's book *Encyclopedia of Furniture Making*, he conducted an

De Facto Apprenticeship

There are no anointed masters, apprentices or journeymen at the Irion Company in Christiana, Pennsylvania. Nevertheless, learning takes place on the job, through an osmotic process that may come as close to traditional apprenticeship as anything that goes by the name today. Irion specializes in custom-built reproduction furniture. They use broad flitches of Western walnut, local cherry and tiger maple in their tables and case goods, and they take pains to apply all the right details and hand-tooled features. "The key to 18th-century furniture making is dovetails," Bert Irion says. "You have to be proficient and you have to be quick. You have to be able to make the furniture *and* make a living. It's very easy to price yourself out of this market."

Irion learned woodworking from his father, and he started the company in 1977. Now, Irion manages the business, procures and selects lumber, and Chris Arato (shown below) is in charge of the shop. Few employees have been formally trained, but all are encouraged to develop their skills by working on their own projects. They set their own hours—there is no time clock—and the shop is available evenings and on weekends. Irion often provides wood at no charge. "Part of what keeps them here is the work and the opportunity to move up," Irion says. "But if their work isn't up to snuff, they'll tread water until it is."

Gerald Martin (shown above right) was a quick study. He joined the company almost eight years ago, with four years of experience in a Virginia cabinetshop. But his work was so rough that Irion started him stripping and sanding furniture, sweeping floors and making deliveries. After six months he began doing repairs and then graduated to making stools, benches and small tables. His big break came literally by accident, when one of the other cabinetmakers maimed his hand on the table saw and Martin stepped in to meet the deadline. "Good for me, bad for him," says Martin.

"Gerald is the company workhorse," Arato says. Martin recently finished four blockfront chests and spent 14 hours dovetailing drawers the day before my visit. A hastily scribbled list of pieces he built last year fills both sides of an envelope and reads like an estate inventory: 23 chests and lowboys, 8 high chests, 40 chairs, and assorted mirrors, night stands and tables. "I took a lot of time off last summer, too," Martin adds.

"It's not that hard to make this furniture," Irion says, "but it *does* take time [to learn]." The skills can be acquired at a number of fine craft schools, but when Irion hires "educated" woodworkers he's usually disappointed. "It's like reading the last chapter of a book first, and then going back to read the rest," he explains. "They come out thinking

The Irion Company has developed a stable of fine cabinetmakers under the supervision of Chris Arato. Here, Arato puts the finishing touches on a Newport blockfront mahogany secretary, reproduced after an original at Rhode Island School of Design.

Gerald Martin (left) and Mike Vesey (right) share a small bench room at the Irion shop in Paoli, Pennsylvania. Vesey is the latest employee to join the company, and Martin is breaking him in in the usual way, with lots of dovetails and hand-planed sides. 'Everybody pays their dues,' Vesey says.

This Philadelphia slant-lid desk and bookcase, built by cabinetmaker Charles Bender in the Irion shop (the original was built between 1760 and 1775), is made of tiger maple and poplar, with carved flame finials and book-matched panels and drawer fronts. The desk lid and panels are from the same set of lumber. (Courtesy Irion Co. Furniture Makers.)

they're cabinetmakers, but the fundamentals just aren't there." Irion has also hired 18-year-olds straight out of high school as well as mature, career-change types, but he prefers young, unmarried workers with some trade experience and no distractions. Some of his most successful hires came out of vocational-training programs.

The work itself can be the best teacher. Before Arato started building the Newport secretary shown on the facing page, he and Martin and Mike Vesey (a new employee who works closely with Martin) set off to Rhode Island to study the original. Measuring and drawing such a sophisticated piece and then figuring out how to quote it and build it would amount to a master's thesis for most woodworkers; the result would demonstrate their grasp of proportion, design and construction. Like much of the work that comes out of the shop, the actual building was a collaboration. One fellow carved the shells, another dovetailed the drawers and a third made the hardware. "I put it together," Arato says, "but everyone has had input."

Doling out responsibility pays off. Irion figures he has five or six de facto "masters" in the shop, any one of whom can make a measured drawing from a photo of a complicated 18th-century piece and then build it. To get to that point isn't easy, but as far as Irion is concerned, "The best thing you can do is find a good shop that's willing to train you." The rest is practice.

During the first three months of his Baulines apprenticeship, Mason Rapaport built the cherry tool chest at left. He completed the coffee table shown below before the end of his term, using vacuum pressure to laminate plywood and veneer over U-shaped plywood ribs. (Photo at left by Roger Heitzman; photo below by Peter Taylor.)

early-morning seminar twice a week, covering everything from shop safety to bent lamination — 23 different topics in all during the course of Rapaport's stay. But Heitzman didn't dwell on the basics. "There are a lot more esoteric skills I like to show," he says, not to mention the countless little time-saving tips gleaned from his years in the trade. "When I think about what Mason knows after being here only six months," Heitzman says, "it's almost unfair."

In the normal ebb and flow of shop work, the balance shifted between the master's and apprentice's projects. Rapaport spent about six weeks in the first three months building the dovetailed cherry tool chest shown at left. He had been planning to make a jewelry box, but Heitzman suggested something more like furniture. Interrupting his work on a desk, Heitzman would summon Rapaport to describe how the legs were attached and to demonstrate a router jig he used to fit them. When Heitzman had a stressful white-lacquered kitchen job to complete, he paid Rapaport as an employee just to crank the work out.

According to Michael Gerlach, Heitzman's regular employee, "Mason was involved in a lot of cool work, some of the best stuff that goes on in the shop." Although employees often receive different treatment than an apprentice — Carpenter told me he always gave his employee the most tedious, repetitive jobs — Gerlach worked closely with Rapaport and provided a production perspective that Heitzman lacked. You might expect some friction to develop between an employee and an apprentice, but Gerlach and Rapaport enjoyed the experience. In fact, Heitzman adds, "I think Mike appreciated not being the bottom man."

Heitzman is an avid machine wizard and he does breathtaking things with the router and with laminated Art Nouveau curves. When Rapaport saw Heitzman's vacuum veneer press in action, he thought, "This is unbelievable — I have

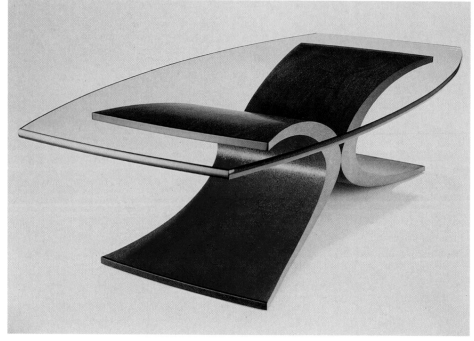

David Marks (at far right) takes a break with his Baulines apprentice Frank Highly and employee Gwen Rosewater. Rosewater and Marks collaborated on the 'Ancient Egyptian Inspired Table' (shown at bottom). Made of mahogany, ebony, fossilized walrus ivory, lapis lazuli, 23-karat gold leaf, patinated copper leaf and faux lapis, the table measures 16 in. x 18 in. x 71 in. Below, Rosewater finishes the details on the carved duck feet. (Photo at at bottom by David J. Marks.)

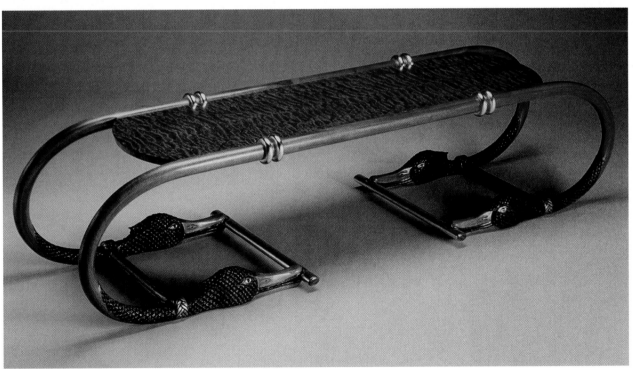

Throughout his apprenticeship to David Marks in Santa Rosa, California, Frank Highly focused on inlay, like the Egyptian-inspired design on this panel.

to try it." With Heitzman's help, Rapaport designed the coffee table shown on p. 177 and laminated it out of four 1/16-in. layers of Finnish birch plywood wrapped around 11 bent plywood ribs. (The whole thing is sheathed in quilted mahogany veneer, with an inlaid ebony border.) The project consumed roughly half of his time—and much of his enthusiasm—during the last three months of his six-month tenure. It was featured in the guild's annual California Design show and sold for $2,000.

Cruising on this "jet assist," Rapaport returned to Lake George, where his father, Myron, recalls, "You couldn't wipe off his grin for a week." The elder Rapaport reckons the experience was "a good graduate-school investment," although he notes wryly that the sale of the coffee table was only a down payment on the total cost. When I visited

the Rapaports after the conclusion of the apprenticeship, Mason was spinning off the coffee-table design into some end tables, a desk and a music stand. Hoping to keep the momentum, he said, "I've only been in this for six months or so, but I've come so far." Heitzman says simply, "I wish I'd had this opportunity when I was getting started."

Several hours north of Heitzman's shop, in Santa Rosa, I visited another guild master who had experimented with several different kinds of apprenticeship. "It gets lonely out here by myself," David Marks told me, and he enjoys having company in the shop. What's more, he says, "it helps me organize my thoughts." Marks was two months into his third BCG apprenticeship when I stopped by. He'd had one previous apprentice through the "Workwise" program of workers' compensation, and two more through a veterans' rehabilitation program.

A full-time employee, Gwen Rosewater, went through an informal six-month apprenticeship in Marks's shop. (Rosewater and Marks collaborated on the "Ancient Egyptian Inspired Table" shown on p. 177.) Rosewater couldn't afford the BCG tuition, so they struck a deal. Marks hired her part time and paid her just enough to activate workers'-compensation insurance. If you look hard enough, he explains, "There are creative ways around the system."

"There's no way you can learn the trade in three months," Marks says, "so whatever I'm working on is what they'll be learning about." But at the time of my visit, BCG apprentice Frank Highly was more interested in doing inlay on his own projects (see the photo on the facing page) than in working on Marks's stuff. By focusing almost entirely on inlay, Highly was able to learn a lot — "as much in three months," Marks figures, "as some people might learn in years." Highly was also exposed to the daily operation of the business: expenses, lumber suppliers and clients. "It's an eye opener," Highly says, and it fosters good communication between master and apprentice. "If you don't tell the apprentices about money and you're making a $7,000 piece," Marks explains, "they think you're getting rich off them."

Roger Heitzman told me that the Baulines apprenticeship program is ideal for people "who are single, can relocate and who have some money." What happens to all those who don't fit that profile? When I spoke with David Marks again, nine months after my visit, he had two new apprentices in the shop, sponsored by the Apprentice Alliance of San Francisco. In the Alliance program, an apprentice pays nothing to the master and receives no money in return. The only costs are the annual membership dues and a $100 matchmaking fee, paid by both parties. Founded in 1978, the Apprentice Alliance has sponsored more than 3,000 apprenticeships in everything from food catering and law to the arts and trades. Its 1991 Directory lists eight woodworking masters.

"Apprentice Alliance is less structured than the BCG," Marks says, and it follows that his new nonpaying apprentices have less to say about what they do. They mainly work for him rather than on their own projects, which allows Marks to concentrate on working more than teaching. He keeps them on a flexible schedule and expects them to stay much longer than his former BCG apprentices. Apart from the cost, perhaps the most tangible difference between the two programs is that the Apprentice Alliance does not provide workers' comp for its apprentices or a teaching stipend for its masters. Marks supplies his own insurance coverage, as he did for Rosewater, and he figures the monthly BCG stipend he received for Highly didn't really cover his time anyway.

Marks and his new apprentices seem satisfied by the present arrangement, but I wondered how a free-labor exchange might affect the master/apprentice relationship. Art Carpenter told me that he used to accept novices on a "nothing/nothing" basis — no money changed hands in either direction. "You want to learn?" he'd ask. "Stick around and I'll have you doing all sorts of things." In the end, he reports, either he or they felt ripped off. "There's no commitment if you don't pay a buck," Carpenter argues. "And if you do receive something, you feel as though you ought to give them something for it."

Apprenticeship by the Sea

In Norway, I'm told, traditional watercraft were built almost entirely by eye. An experienced craftsman could make a good 20-ft. faering in a week, without plans, molds or lofting (the practice of sketching the full-scale lines of a boat on the shop floor). A keel is stretched, the garboards are hung and the sides are planked. Then the knees are shaped and riveted inside the planks for reinforcement and to maintain the shape of the hull.

That kind of skill doesn't come from a book or a classroom, and if you thought it arcane you'd be almost right. A few years ago, the Apprenticeshop in Rockport, Maine, sent two of their own to Norway to learn how to build a boat the old way. According to the Apprenticeshop's founder, Lance Lee, the Norwegians themselves had only recently revived the tradition.

Restoring traditional skills is at the heart of modern apprenticeship, and Lee has been tinkering with the model for most of his life. He has worked in and around boats since his childhood in the Bahamas, but Lee's concept of apprenticeship coalesced during the nine months he spent at sea in 1970, grappling with 12 miles of rigging under the able tutelage of a Norwegian boatswain. They spoke different languages, but Lee says, "I came away knowing that physical skills are one of the most remarkable forces for continuity." Imbued with the experiential philosophy of Outward Bound, where he'd been an instructor, Lee set out to develop a program of traditional hand skills that would pair the energy and time of young people with the experience of their elders. Building boats was a natural.

The first Apprenticeshop was built in 1972 on the Kennebec River in Bath, and it was a part of the Maine Maritime Museum. Bath was home to half of the American merchant fleet at the turn of the century, and a 1891 journal noted that "a Bath man can no more help building ships than he can help breathing." Of course, those days were long gone, and the sole remaining shipyard on the Kennebec River — Bath Iron Works — was not exactly ripe for a wooden-boat revival.

Lee anguished over the term "apprenticeship." He'd been warned by an English master builder that it was pointless to teach boatbuilders over 15 years old, but Lee knew that an old-fashioned apprenticeship would fail for lack of enrollment and funding. What's more, he was not interested in training merely "right-handed, technical-vocational boatbuilders." The decision Lee made then has guided everything he's done since: Boats were the vehicle and people would be the product.

People trickled in. It was a small enough crew to begin with — five apprentices, plus Lee and his wife Dorothy — and they gathered once a week around Lee's table for a ritual meal. Before they laid their first keel, the apprentices dismantled seven old barns and recycled the materials into a two and one-half story boatshop. They built a series of bateaux, knocked together quickly for a reenactment of the Battle of

apprentices is to solve enough of their food, clothing and tool problems so they can dedicate themselves to the task."

The Apprenticeshop thrived and Lee introduced a six-week paying internship and a volunteer program, which would take care of the shop and grounds. Apprentices were paired with interns and had to teach the skills they'd just learned. Their newfound enthusiasm put them in an ideal position to pass it on. "Plus, you learn it better if you have to teach it," Lee explains. Admissions and graduations were staggered, so that senior apprentices would be able to work with newcomers. It was a heady time and, by 1978, there were so many applicants that they opened the Restoration Shop downriver, on the former site of a 19th-century shipyard. The two shops shared tools, planked boats in relays and passed overflow orders between them. They ran joint expeditions up and down the coast, toting fish and fiberglass resin.

Ten years and about 100 boats after the first bateaux, Lee ran afoul of the trustees. He was fired, and the original building was closed in 1982. (The Maine Maritime Museum took over the Restoration Shop, which continues to operate its own apprenticeship program.) While the rest of the crew went off to lick their wounds, Lee hunted for a new home. Within days, he had a site in Rockport and orders for 11 boats. He would begin where he left off, with "one good boat built uncompromisingly after another." But to distinguish Rockport from Bath, Lee wanted the new shop to become "an emporium of international exchange." He began to recruit apprentices and instructors from all over the world.

Lee has never ducked controversy. In 20 years and three different boat shops, his vision of apprenticeship has been called romantic, and his apprentices have been called misfits, slowpokes and worse. "We've lived with that stigma," he says, but he makes no apologies. Most of the roughly 180 graduates, Lee figures, are working in the industry, but he's equally as proud of the rest: Charlie's a cabinetmaker, Rex is a lawyer, Anna makes violas. A handful—four or five by Lee's own account—have become first-quality boatbuilders. "Master craftsmen will always be rare," Lee says. "They will be 'cursed' to go on and be more and more specialized. Their curse is our blessing. A great many other people will be more inclined to use their hands."

Lance Lee and Perseverance, *the 26-ft. sail-training vessel that has been used all over New England to train apprentices. The lines of the boat were taken off of a 19th-century Penobscot Bay pinky schooner. Its keel was laid on the first day Lee opened the Rockport Apprenticeshop.*

Quebec. These were followed by overbuilt dories, "as good as the bateaux were bad," Lee says, adding with a rascal grin, "The dory resembles apprenticeship—the more you load it, the more stable it rides."

The core of the program was a two-year boatbuilding apprenticeship, and the only tuition was labor (around the shop and living quarters, as well as on the boats). Apprentices lived and ate together and shared decisions about running the shop. The kids who had to moonlight to make ends meet were the most resilient—and the most exhausted. In a throwback to tradition, Lee says, "The best favor you can do for your

The Rockport and Bath Apprenticeshops are perhaps the most visible boatbuilding programs in Maine, but they are not alone. From Kennebunk to the Canadian border, there are at least seven or eight different boat schools, not counting informal backyard arrangements or the more structured trade programs to be found in some shipyards. *WoodenBoat* magazine maintains a list of more than 30 active boatbuilding programs across the United States and Canada, with seven more in England.

That list does not yet include Lee's latest enterprise, a new shop he calls Atlantic Challenge, which began with the construction of two 38-ft. French-American rowing and sailing gigs. (Built in Rockport and in France, the gigs were launched in a ceremonial contest of seamanship at the 1986 anniversary of the Statue of Liberty.) Retooling his concept to encompass seamanship as well as traditional boatbuilding, Lee now sees apprenticeship as a lingua franca for international communication. Shops have been built or are being planned in eight member nations, and teams of

apprentices are building boats in each others' shops and sailing them together.

In pursuit of the dream, Lee recently parted company with the Rockport Apprenticeshop and established his fourth boatshop in an old mill not far from Rockport. While Lee heads for uncharted water, Rockport seems to be steering towards the mainstream of vocational boatbuilding. Rockport's new associate director, Ben Fuller, told me he hoped to incorporate more modern technologies (like cold molding), and he wanted to be sure apprentices got a good introduction to the power tools they might encounter in a professional shop. They are also keeping track of time and materials and have begun to negotiate their own material purchases. As Rockport rededicates itself to the training of boatbuilders, Fuller says, "whatever detracts from the learning experience" will have to go.

Apprentice Bill Bichell gets out a mast in the Rockport Apprenticeshop. After completing the Rockport program, Bichell went on to teach boatbuilding at the Sound School in New Haven and at the Maritime Center in South Norwalk, Connecticut, before returning to teach at the Apprenticeshop.

This three-masted, 38-ft. Bantry Bay gig is the first boat to be built at the new Atlantic Challenge shop in Nobleboro, Maine. The multinational crew is (from left to right): instructor Dario Bravi (Italy) with apprentices Fung Lim (Singapore), Artyem Dubinine (Russia), James Gregg (United States) and Mischa Plekanov (Russia). (Photo by Carla Dolloff.)

Lee's Atlantic Challenge is a leaner, tighter "demonstrator" model, designed to spawn Apprenticeshops all over the world. In addition to the 38-ft., three-masted Bantry Bay being built at the new shop (shown above) boats are currently underway in Wales and in Canada. Thinking back to the Norwegian faering, Lee says, "I want to do it again and again and again — in Spain and Portugal, in France and in Pakistan." In August of 1991, watching the moon rise over the Neva River, Lee helped lay the cornerstone for the first Russian Apprenticeshop.

Endings and Beginnings

Whether Lance Lee is watering down the institution of apprenticeship or plugging the dike with his thumb is a matter of debate. In either case, he's not alone. I keep finding new examples of homegrown apprenticeships and institutional training programs. A recent issue of *Fine Woodworking* magazine lists more than 200 schools and workshops that offer training in woodworking. Many states also

collaborate with trade unions and industry to provide a form of vocational training that is rooted in apprenticeship. In difficult economic times, we may look increasingly to these institutional models as a tool for resuscitating American industry.

Vocational training and art schools have their place, but artisans — not institutions — are the traditional keepers of the "mystery and art" of woodworking. Art and craft were absorbed by the schools at about the same time that production moved into the factory and social welfare was taken over by government. But they needn't remain there. As potter Gerry Williams asserted in his book, *Apprenticeship In Craft,* "I want universities to give back what was ours to start with: the master's degree." One apprentice I met took a more pragmatic approach to the problem: "The money I'd spend in school could equip a small shop."

As long as apprenticeship is conducted informally, there will always be abuses. (There were plenty even when the English guilds were enforcing the artificer's statutes.) After all, what's to stop any wood butcher with extra bench space and a few seminars under his belt from hanging out his master's shingle? In theory, nothing. In reality, there's the law. In 1974, Simon Watts discovered that even the most honorable of intentions can be derailed by the government. Watts had been accepting apprentices in his Vermont cabinetshop for years before he began charging tuition to account for his time.

The arrangement worked fine, and Watts was never short of applicants, until the United States Department of Labor charged him with violation of the Fair Labor Standards Act of 1938. Because his apprentices worked on furniture that Watts sold for a profit, they were considered employees and were therefore entitled to a minimum wage. If Watts was forced to pay the $13,000 of back wages the government said he owed, he would lose the shop.

Watts hired a lawyer. He did not question the government's obligation to protect workers from unscrupulous employers, but simply argued that the laws were too restrictive and that his financial gain was more than offset by the time he spent teaching. "We beat it," Watts says, although it cost him a desk in payment to his attorney. Many other would-be masters might prefer to avoid a situation with so many legal ambiguities, but Watts never stopped taking apprentices. (He did insist that they carry their own accident and medical insurance.) "I am convinced," Watts wrote at the time, "that a proper apprentice program is an excellent way to acquire most manual skills."

Apprenticeship ends in many ways. As Gerry Williams observed, "There are two factors that often cause friction in the workshop: psychological incompatibility of the master and apprentice, and failure on the part of the master to allow the apprentice to grow." Growth can be built into an agreement, as in a graduated wage scale or in the expectation that an apprentice will spend less time on the master's work as he or she gains experience.

But a successful apprenticeship has always been much more than a tight contract. Apprentices and masters are engaged in a dynamic balancing act — trying to satisfy the interests of both parties while keeping a business afloat. As long as they appreciate the value of the exchange, the relationship stands a reasonable chance of success. When they don't, it's unlikely to survive.

Money is not the same as value, and paying a large tuition will not guarantee that an apprentice receives more information or a more knowledgeable master, although it usually buys more control over the experience. Generally, the more apprentices pay, the more they can expect to work on their own projects or get direct instruction from their master. Whatever support a master offers an apprentice — in the form of wages, stipends, lodging, or access to tools and materials — generally buys labor.

It's questionable how much this arrangement really benefits the modern master. If sheer volume or quality of work were the only criteria, most woodworkers would do better on their own. But many masters yearn to belong to something larger than themselves. As Simon Watts explains, they are sharing "not just the experience of one man, but the accumulated experience of generations."

Lawyer and chairmaker John Alexander, Jr., recalls his apprentice this way: "Gelli would come down and watch and sweep and tote." Alexander works a lot with green wood and he found that "as the woodworking got wetter, Gelli became more useful," One day the apprentice surprised Alexander with a completed chair that he'd built entirely on his own. "He learned how to build that chair by osmosis," Alexander says. "It happened gradually...and it ended gradually. And then we gave him his tools," says Alexander, adding after a slight pause, "I'd still like to get that drawknife back!"

(Courtesy The Winterthur Library: Printed Book and Periodical Collection.)

Index

Publisher: *John Kelsey*
Editor: *Andy Schultz*
Associate editor: *Sandor Nagyszalanczy*
Designer/layout artist: *Jodie Delohery*
Copy/production editor: *Pam Purrone*

Typeface: ITC Garamond Light
Paper: Silverado Gloss, 80lb., neutral pH
Printer and binder: Ringier America, New Berlin, Wisconsin